THE ODYSSEY

Adapted and abridged by Andrew Biliter

Based on the epic
by Homer

WANT TO PERFORM THIS PLAY? YOU NEED TO GET THE RIGHTS!

But don't worry, it's easy. We have affordable licensing options for any size organization, and we'll get your contract finalized in just a few days.

Questions?
info@lighthouseplays.com
(872) 228-7826
lighthouseplays.com

CAST OF CHARACTERS

Greek Warriors returning from Troy
   ODYSSEUS, King of Ithaca
   EURYLOCHUS, the first mate
   ELPENOR, the lookout
   PERMENIDES
   MNESTHEUS
   DOLIUS
   MINNOW
   MAKAR
   ANTIPHUS
   POLITES

People of Ithaca
   PENELOPE, wife of Oysseus
   YOUNG TELEMACHUS, son of Odysseus at age 9
   TELEMACHUS as a teenager
   ANTICLEA, mother of Odysseus
   EUMAEUS, the loyal swineherd
   EURYCLEIA, handmaid to Penelope
   ELENI, a servant girl, playmate to Young Telemachus
   PEISANDER, a servant
   PHEMIOS, a bard
   PHOEBE, a servant
   A **TRAVELER** visiting Ithaca
   A **SOOTHSAYER**

Gods, Creatures, and Prophets
   ATHENA, goddess of wisdom
   AEOLUS, god of the winds
   CALYPSO the nymph
   CIRCE the enchantress
   TIRESIAS the prophet
   The **CYCLOPS** Polyphemus (Voice)
   NEIGHBOR Cyclops (Voice)
   INO the sea nymph
   An **EMISSARY** from the Underworld

Suitors to Penelope
ANTINOUS, the head suitor
NOEMON, the tall suitor
EURYMACHUS, the lean suitor
THOAS
BIAS
LEOCRITUS
POLYBUS
ELATUS

Ensemble Roles
Cannibals, Lotus Eaters, Sheep, Sirens, Circe's Handmaids, Tentacles of Charybdis, Spirits of the Underworld, Waves of Poseidon, Servant Girls

SUGGESTED DOUBLING

With over forty speaking roles in the script, there are many ways to do doubling. Here is how it was done in the original production for a cast of 26. Further condensing is certainly possible.

ODYSSEUS
PENELOPE
ATHENA
YOUNG TELEMACHUS
TELEMACHUS
CALYPSO / Traveler / Ensemble
CIRCE / Ensemble
TIRESIAS the prophet / Ensemble
ANTICLEA, mother of Odysseus / Ensemble
EUMAEUS the swineherd / Cyclops (voice)
EURYCLEIA, handmaid to Penelope / Ensemble
AEOLUS, god of wind / ANTINOUS, the head suitor
NOEMON, the tall suitor / Neighbor Cyclops
EURYMACHUS, the lean suitor
EURYLOCHUS, the first mate / BIAS, a suitor
ELPENOR, the lookout / THOAS, a suitor
PERMENIDES, a sailor / Soothsayer of Ithaca
MNESTHEUS, a sailor / PEISANDER, a servant
DOLIUS, a sailor / PHEMIOS, a bard
MINNOW, a sailor / Ensemble
MAKAR, a sailor / LEOCRITUS, a suitor
ANTIPHUS, a sailor / POLYBUS, a suitor
POLITES, a sailor / ELATUS, a suitor
ELENI, a servant girl / Ensemble
INO the sea nymph / Ensemble
PHOEBE, a servant / Ensemble

ACT 1, SCENE 1

"Prologue"

Ithaca, an open place.

*Enter ELENI and YOUNG TELEMACHUS, with wooden swords.
EUMAEUS the swineherd watches from a distance.*

ELENI. I will no longer fly you, Achilles. Let me either slay or be slain!

YOUNG TELEMACHUS. Good. At last may I see the great Hector put forth all his strength!

They duel. ELENI pulls away.

ELENI. A covenant first! Let us agree that whichever man wins, he shall treat his rival's body with respect.

YOUNG TELEMACHUS. Fool, speak not to me of covenants. Wolves and lambs can never be of one mind, but must hate each other through and through. This is for my cousin!

He charges at her but she dodges and deflects him. He stumbles.

ELENI. You have missed your aim, Achilles. Perhaps the gods do not favor you as much as you claim. And now you must avoid me.

She attacks furiously, leaping and soaring like an eagle.

Enter EURYCLEIA. At the sound of her voice, EUMAEUS shrinks into the shadows.

EURYCLEIA. Eleni!

ELENI. Uh oh.

EURYCLEIA. What are you doing out here? You're supposed to be milking the goats!

ELENI. Sorry, miss.

EURYCLEIA. Master Telemachus, I know you're very fond of sport, but can't you find any other child to play with? Eleni has chores.

YOUNG TELEMACHUS. But we weren't playing, Eurycleia; we were having a lesson.

EURYCLEIA. A lesson, is it? (*realizing who it must be*) Where's that swineherd? Eumaeus!

EUMAEUS (*stepping out from hiding*). Here.

EURYCLEIA. Did you put them up to this?

EUMAEUS. Aye, miss. We've been re-enacting the great battles at Troy. It's a lesson in tactics!

EURYCLEIA. And what does a serving girl want with a lesson in tactics?

YOUNG TELEMACHUS. Please, Eurycleia. None of the boys can fight as well as Eleni.

EURYCLEIA. Oh, very well. But goats after!

ELENI. Yes, miss! (*snapping back into character*) Die, Achilles!

> *They resume fighting with all the energy they had before.*

EUMAEUS. Good, lads! (*to EURYCLEIA*) Eurycleia, stay and watch a bit.

EURYCLEIA. I haven't time.

EUMAEUS. Oh, but it's the most exciting bit, see? Hector of Troy fancies himself invincible because he stole Achilles' armor. But Achilles knows that armor as he knows his own skin. He knows all the weak points, see? So he takes aim... and STRIKES!

> *YOUNG TELEMACHUS pretends to stab ELENI in the breastplate. She falls to her knees.*

ELENI. Please, a proper burial. I beg you.

YOUNG TELEMACHUS. After what you did to Patroclus? Never. The dogs and vultures will have you now.

ELENI. Please...

EUMAEUS. And then brave Achilles ties the body of Hector to his chariot and drags it round and round the city walls.

YOUNG TELEMACHUS takes ELENI on his back and marches in a circle.

YOUNG TELEMACHUS. Glory to Greece! Glory to the gods!

EUMAEUS. Well?

ELENI. Wasn't it thrilling?

YOUNG TELEMACHUS. Wasn't it epic?

EURYCLEIA. I don't understand why men go to war. Come along, Eleni.

ALL. Awwww!

Exit all except YOUNG TELEMACHUS.

Alone he continues to play as both Hector and Achilles.

YOUNG TELEMACHUS (*lying down*). "A proper burial. I beg you." (*getting up*) "After what you did to Patroclus? Never."

Enter ATHENA.

ATHENA. Aren't you going to show how it ended?

YOUNG TELEMACHUS. How what ended?

ATHENA. Troy. The war.

YOUNG TELEMACHUS. That story is all anybody knows. A sailor came to Ithaca and told us the story a year ago.

ATHENA. Oh, but so much has happened since then! Achilles had defeated Hector, yes, but Troy still stood. Its walls were strong, and the Greeks had no way of breaching them. But then, in the tenth year of the siege, one of the Greeks came up with a plan. He said, "Let's fool the Trojans!" We'll take apart our ships, and build a wooden horse of mountainous size. We'll place it before the city gates, with thirty of our best warriors crouched inside. The Greeks did as he said, and in the morning the Trojans awoke to find the Greek encampment gone and a giant horse standing at their doorstep. Overjoyed, they wheeled the horse inside. But when night fell, the Greeks climbed out of the horse and sacked the city, burning it to the ground. That's how the war was won.

YOUNG TELEMACHUS. I don't believe it.

ATHENA. Believe what you want. It all happened, just as I say.

YOUNG TELEMACHUS. But how do you know?

ATHENA. Because I was just there.

YOUNG TELEMACHUS. You were there and now you're here?

ATHENA. I travel fast.

YOUNG TELEMACHUS. And tell me, traveler: did you see my father, Odysseus?

ATHENA. Haven't you guessed it yet? It was your father who devised the Trojan Horse. He was the real hero of Troy.

YOUNG TELEMACHUS. I knew it!

ATHENA. Clearly you didn't.

YOUNG TELEMACHUS. I have to run and tell Mother! Father is coming home! I'll get to meet him for the first time since I was a baby!

ATHENA. Don't be so sure of that, child. The war may be over, but I have come to tell you that your father still has a long journey ahead of him.

YOUNG TELEMACHUS. I don't think so.

ATHENA. Don't you?

YOUNG TELEMACHUS. No. You see, I know my father.

ATHENA. Do you?

YOUNG TELEMACHUS. Well, not personally, but Mother has told me all about him! And if what she told me is true, then nothing will stop him from coming home.

ATHENA. What did she tell you?

YOUNG TELEMACHUS. That he's the bravest, strongest, cleverest man who ever lived!

> *They exit.*

ACT 1, SCENE 2
"The Lotus Eaters"

Enter ODYSSEUS and ten SAILORS, pursued by CANNIBALS.

ODYSSEUS. Run! Run for your lives! Get to the ship!

The CANNIBALS stand at the water's edge, shouting, snarling, and pointing their spears at the SAILORS.

FIRST CANNIBAL. Stay!

SECOND CANNIBAL. You're just in time for lunch!

THIRD CANNIBAL. Come back, morsels!

PERMENIDES. Get off me!

EURYLOCHUS. Take the oars!

ODYSSEUS. Permenides, you fool! Don't try to fight them, just get to your post!

The SAILORS get to their places and take up their oars.

EURYLOCHUS. Row, row!

The snarling CANNIBALS recede into the distance.

ELPENOR. Phew! I think we're safe now.

ODYSSEUS. Eurylochus, are all the men accounted for?

EURYLOCHUS. Aye, Captain.

ODYSSEUS. Was anyone bitten?

PERMENIDES. I was, Captain, but not badly.

EURYLOCHUS. Captain?

ODYSSEUS. What?

EURYLOCHUS. You said the Laestrygonians would be friendly.

ODYSSEUS. Well, they were! They just also happened to be... cannibals.

EURYLOCHUS. And so will we be soon if we don't find food!

ELPENOR. Land ho!

ODYSSEUS. Already?

ELPENOR. Yes, Captain. I see a large island, lush with vegetation! Looks uninhabited.

ODYSSEUS. Excellent. We'll make landfall on that beach.

EURYLOCHUS. Port side, fall out.

DOLIUS. I hope there are figs.

EURYLOCHUS. Easy oars!

MNESTHEUS. Figs? Ha! I hope there's wild boar to eat.

EURYLOCHUS. Brace!

> *The ship hits the beach.*

MNESTHEUS. Last one off the ship is a mama's boy!

ODYSSEUS. Hold! I've learned my lesson having everyone go at once. We'll send a scouting party first. Eurylochus, you lead it. Take Makar, Elpenor, and Minnow with you.

EURYLOCHUS. Aye, Captain.

ODYSSEUS. And this time, if you meet anyone, treat them with courtesy. We are not in Troy anymore, understand? No pillaging.

EURYLOCHUS. Understood, Captain.

> *Exit EURYLOCHUS, MAKAR, ELPENOR, and MINNOW.*

> *The remaining SAILORS sit down to wait.*

ODYSSEUS. Don't get too comfortable, sailors. It's a small island. I doubt it will take long to survey.

> *Lights down and quickly up again. SAILORS are in a new waiting tableau, a bit more miserable than before.*

ODYSSEUS. Can't be much longer.

> *Lights down and quickly up again. SAILORS are in a new waiting tableau, even more miserable.*

ODYSSEUS. Just a bit longer. The island must be larger than it seems.

> *Lights down and quickly up again. SAILORS are at death's door.*

PERMENIDES. Captain, I am melting. It's been hours!

ODYSSEUS. You're right. It's been too long. We'd better go find them. Dolius, Permenides, and Antiphus, come with me. The rest of you stay here.

> *Remaining SAILORS groan. ODYSSEUS, DOLIUS, ANTIPHUS, and PERMENIDES follow the path the other SAILORS took as the remaining SAILORS strike the sail and exit.*

> *Scene transition: A lotus tree appears. It is hung with golden, glowing fruit. Around it lounge the LOTUS EATERS, along with EURYLOCHUS, MAKAR, ELPENOR, and MINNOW. They are all smiling serenely.*

ODYSSEUS. Eurylochus!

EURYLOCHUS. Mmm?

ODYSSEUS. Eurylochus, what are you doing? We've all been waiting for you on the beach.

EURYLOCHUS. Oh… They've been waiting for us on the beach.

ELPENOR. Really? They should come visit!

MINNOW. Yes, they should. It's lovely here, you know.

MAKAR. Far better than THERE.

MINNOW. Come sit with us.

LOTUS EATERS. Yes. Please do…

ODYSSEUS. There's no time for sitting. We need to be gathering food and water so we can set sail for Ithaca.

> *Pause.*

EURYLOCHUS. Why?

ODYSSEUS. What do you mean, why?

EURYLOCHUS. Why go to Ithaca? Why struggle day after day?

MINNOW. Because, when you think about it, what IS Ithaca?

ELPENOR. It's a rock.

MINNOW. Yes!

ELPENOR. A rock jutting out of the sea, just like this one. Only that one is far away, and this one we are already on!

MAKAR. And who is to say that this place ISN'T Ithaca?

MINNOW. Right. Ithaca is wherever we decide it is.

ODYSSEUS. No it isn't!

MINNOW. He doesn't understand.

> *They laugh.*

EURYLOCHUS. Here. Try this and you'll know what we mean.

ODYSSEUS. What is it?

ELPENOR. "What is it?" (*laughs*) It's only the lotus fruit, the most perfect food on Earth.

EURYLOCHUS. See how it glows?

MAKAR. Really, you must try it.

MINNOW. Nothing else compares!

FIRST LOTUS EATER. Come dine with us!

SECOND LOTUS EATER. Recline with us,

THIRD LOTUS EATER. Unwind with us and eat the lotus.

FOURTH LOTUS EATER. Forget your homes and families as we have.

FIRST LOTUS EATER. Forget sorrow.

SECOND LOTUS EATER. Forget pain.

THIRD LOTUS EATER. Linger here.

FOURTH LOTUS EATER. Taste, and forget!

Entranced, ANTIPHUS starts reaching for the fruit.

ODYSSEUS. Antiphus, don't eat that!

ANTIPHUS. But it smells so good!

ODYSSEUS. Come here, all of you.

DOLIUS, PERMENIDES, and ANTIPHUS gather round ODYSSEUS.

DOLIUS. What is it, Captain?

ODYSSEUS. This is a cursed place. We need to get our men out of here NOW.

PERMENIDES. Can't you just order them back to the ship?

ODYSSEUS. Too late for that. We'll have to take them by surprise. Each of you grab a man and drag him to the ship. And whatever you do, don't touch the fruit. Understood?

SAILORS. Yes, Captain.

ODYSSEUS. On my signal. One. Two. Three!

They each grab a man, causing a terrible ruckus.

MINNOW. What are you doing?

ELPENOR. Stop it!

MAKAR. Let me go!

EURYLOCHUS. Odysseus, no! Please.

PERMENIDES. Drop it!

MINNOW. No! It's mine!

PERMENIDES. Come on.

MINNOW. But I need it! You don't understand! I need it!

The SAILORS are dragged away to the ship. But at the last second, EURYLOCHUS struggles out of ODYSSEUS' arms.

ODYSSEUS. Eurylochus!

EURYLOCHUS (*grabbing a stick*). Stay back! I'm warning you.

ODYSSEUS. Eurylochus, don't do this.

EURYLOCHUS. You can't have my lotus. It's mine!

ODYSSEUS. I don't want your lotus, I want you to come home.

EURYLOCHUS. You keep saying "home." I don't know where that is!

ODYSSEUS. Yes you do. Come on.

He makes a move toward EURYLOCHUS.

EURYLOCHUS. I'll kill you!

EURYLOCHUS springs at ODYSSEUS, and ODYSSEUS knocks him out in one punch.

ODYSSEUS. I'm sorry. I had no choice.

Enter ANTICLEA, in flashback. Light change.

LOTUS EATERS exit.

ANTICLEA. There's always a choice.

ODYSSEUS. Not this time, Mother. Sparta is our ally. I swore to help them.

ANTICLEA. To hell with Sparta! How can you abandon us like this? Your mother? Your wife? Your infant son?

ODYSSEUS. Mother, don't do this.

ANTICLEA. How is he to learn to be king without a father's example?

Enter EURYCLEIA and PENELOPE, with baby bundle in her arms.

ODYSSEUS. You and Penelope will teach him.

ANTICLEA. We can't. We need you. Don't go!

ODYSSEUS. Mother, I'm so sorry.

ANTICLEA. Don't say you're sorry, say you'll stay! Please, I beg you…

She breaks down sobbing.

EURYCLEIA. There, there, Anticlea. Come with me.

EURYCLEIA leads the sobbing ANTICLEA off.

ODYSSEUS. I've never seen her like this.

PENELEOPE. She was like this when your father died.

ODYSSEUS. She doesn't think I'm coming home.

PENELOPE. She's wrong.

ODYSSEUS. How do you know?

PENELOPE. I just know.

ODYSSEUS. What if instead of sailing to Troy you and I just sailed away to a little island and grew old together?

PENELOPE. We could do that… but if we did, then you wouldn't be the honorable man that I married. And I would have no desire for you.

ODYSSEUS chuckles.

PENELOPE. Just remember why these other kings have called on you. They have Achilles for brawn; but they need Odysseus for his wits. So use them. Be clever, for your own sake and for mine. And for Telemachus.

ODYSSEUS. Penelope, if I should die…

PENELOPE. Don't say that.

ODYSSEUS. No, listen. If I should die, you must rule Ithaca until Telemachus is a man. Once he is grown, he will become king, and you can take a new husband.

PENELOPE. But I don't want to be with anyone but you.

ODYSSEUS. Penelope, we're still young. Don't give up on your own life just because mine ends.

PENELOPE. But you're not going to die. You're coming back to me. I'm certain.

ODYSSEUS. I only hope the gods look on me as favorably as you do.

>   *ODYSSEUS moves in for a farewell kiss.*

PENELOPE. Captain, where shall we make landfall?

ODYSSEUS. What?

>   *Scene transition. PENELOPE exits as SAILORS retake their positions onstage.*

ACT 1, SCENE 3
"The Cyclops"

Back on the ship with the SAILORS.

EURYLOCHUS. I said where shall we make landfall?

ODYSSEUS. Oh, uh… that beachhead there.

EURYLOCHUS. Oars up! Brace!

The ship hits the beach.

PERMENIDES. Ooh, look there, Captain! Wild wheat, barley, grapes. This island seems a very hospitable place.

ODYSSEUS. That's what we said about the last island. Let's meet the inhabitants first. Who wants to explore that cave with me?

All the men volunteer enthusiastically except EURYLOCHUS.

ODYSSEUS. Settle down, settle down. Eurylochus, why isn't your hand raised?

EURYLOCHUS. Well, Captain, I'm not sure I trust myself anymore after the lotus fruit incident.

ODYSSEUS. All the more reason for you to come along.

EURYLOCHUS. But Captain—

ODYSSEUS. A first mate who doesn't trust himself is a danger to all of us. Now, I can either promote a new first mate or you can shake it off and come with me.

EURYLOCHUS. I'll come.

ODYSSEUS. Good. Polites, Dolius, Antiphus, and Mnestheus, you come, too. The rest of you, stay here.

ELPENOR. Yes, Captain.

The two groups exit their separate ways. Set change to inside cave.

ODYSSEUS. Hello? Anyone home? (*his voice echoes back*) Let's have a look around.

Inside the cave, the men are overwhelmed by its size and scale.

ANTIPHUS. Whoa…

EURYLOCHUS. Incredible.

POLITES. Have you ever seen such a place?

MNESTHEUS puts his finger to the floor and smells it.

MNESTHEUS. Captain. Sheep dung. Shepherds must live here.

DOLIUS. Who ever heard of penning sheep in a cave?

ANTIPHUS peers inside a large container.

ANTIPHUS. Oh… Aha!

POLITES. What is it, Antiphus?

ANTIPHUS. Cheese! Lots of it!

MNESTHEUS. Ooh, let me try! (*he tastes it*)

POLITES. Well? How is it?

Pause.

MNESTHEUS. Dolius… bring the wine.

The SAILORS cheer and begin gorging on wine and cheese.

EURYLOCHUS. Odysseus, come feast with us!

ODYSSEUS. Oh, why not?

SAILORS. Hooray!

ODYSSEUS. But don't eat ALL the cheese or we may anger our host. Save some wine for him, and then perhaps there will be mutton in our future.

POLITES. Mutton! Oh, excellent!

DOLIUS. You know, I never much cared for shepherds.

ANTIPHUS. Nor I. But now we love them!

DOLIUS. Aye, with all our hearts!

MNESTHEUS. To our host, may his generosity never cease!

SAILORS. To our host!

The sound of earth-shaking footsteps.

EURYLOCHUS. Uh oh.

ODYSSEUS. Mnestheus, go see what that was.

MNESTHEUS cautiously creeps offstage. Sound of a giant boulder being dragged across the ground. The lights dim. MNESTHEUS returns in panic.

ODYSSEUS. Mnestheus, is that you?

MNESTHEUS. Yes, captain!

EURYLOCHUS. What did you see?

MNESTHEUS. I don't know. Someone pushed a giant boulder in front of the cave entrance and then the light went out.

DOLIUS. Oh no, we're trapped!

Sound of footsteps returns, louder.

ANTIPHUS. What do we do?

ODYSSEUS. Hide!

Enter CYCLOPS, represented by a giant eye and two enormous hands, along with a flock of SHEEP, represented by ensemble members with patches of white wool strapped to their backs.

The CYCLOPS hums a happy tune.

CYCLOPS. Run along, sheep, run along. Let's see… A fire is what we need.

He cups his hands around a hearth and fire illuminates the room.

CYCLOPS (*seeing the men*). Strangers? Who are you? Traders, rovers, ne'er-do-wells? Where do you sail from?

ODYSSEUS. We are Greeks on our way home from Troy, but by the will of the gods, we have been driven off course. We humbly beg your hospitality.

CYCLOPS. And why should I give it?

ODYSSEUS. Well, as you know, the gods protect all travelers.

CYCLOPS. Fool! We Cyclopses do not fear the gods, for we are much stronger than they. Now tell me, where is your vessel?

POLITES. Oh, you didn't see her? She's moored just outside and around the—

ODYSSEUS. Wrecked.

CYCLOPS. What?

ODYSSEUS. It's wrecked. We wrecked it on the rocks east of here, so we had to swim to shore. It's a miracle we're all alive.

CYCLOPS. Saved by the gods, were you?

ALL (*ad lib*). Yes. By the gods, certainly. That's right.

ANTIPHUS. The gods love us!

CYCLOPS. Do they? Well, let's see if they can help you now.

> *CYCLOPS reaches out and grabs ANTIPHUS with his huge hand.*
> *The other SAILORS scream and try to pull him from the CYCLOPS' grip.*

ALL (*ad lib*). Noooooo! Hold on! Hold on, Antiphus!

> *But the CYCLOPS is far stronger than they, and he devours the SAILOR.*
> *The SAILORS weep and lift their hands to heaven, crying, "Why? Why, gods?"*

CYCLOPS. Ahhh. It's been years since I enjoyed the taste of human flesh. Bring me that bucket of milk to wash it down.

ODYSSEUS. Milk? Did you say milk?

CYCLOPS. Milk! And bring it fast or you'll be next.

ODYSSEUS. Forgive me, Cyclops, but human flesh is much better paired with wine.

CYCLOPS. Wine? Huh. Never heard of it!

The SAILORS gasp in astonishment.

ODYSSEUS. Never heard of wine! Why, it's the drink of the gods!

CYCLOPS. I thought they drank nectar.

ODYSSEUS. Trust me, this is better.

The SAILORS agree.

CYCLOPS. And where might I find this "wine?"

ODYSSEUS. Take ours as an offering, that you might take pity on us.

CYCLOPS. It's not poison?

MNESTHEUS. Oh, far from it!

CYCLOPS. All right, let's give it a try then.

Two SAILORS pour some wine into the mouth of the CYCLOPS.

CYCLOPS. Mmm. More!

ODYSSEUS. Give him more.

They give him more.

CYCLOPS. Mmm… That's good. Very good. What is your noble name, human?

ODYSSEUS. My name? Why it's—

EURYLOCHUS. Don't tell him! He could use it against us.

ODYSSEUS (*signaling, "I got this"*). It's Nohb.

CYCLOPS. Nohb?

ODYSSEUS. Yes. Nohb… Adi.

CYCLOPS. Nohb Adi? That's a strange name.

ODYSSEUS. You can take it up with my mother.

CYCLOPS. Ha! Well, Nohb Adi, because of your generosity, I want to give you a gift. I will eat you... last of all.

> *Pause.*

ODYSSEUS. You are too kind.

CYCLOPS. Don't mention it... (*yawning*) Oh, and now I take my rest. Goodnight, my breakfast.

> *The CYCLOPS goes to sleep, snoring.*

EURYLOCHUS. Good thinking, Captain!

DOLIUS. What do we do now?

POLITES. I say we kill him!

ODYSSEUS. No, no, no. We can't kill him. Not yet, at least.

MNESTHEUS. Why not?

ODYSSEUS. Tell them, Eurylochus.

EURYLOCHUS. The stone that blocks the door. He's the only one who can move it. If we kill him, we're stuck.

SAILORS. Ohhhhh.

MNESTHEUS. So, what do we do?

ODYSSEUS (*looking around*). That post. Sharpen the end of it, then hold the point in the fire until it's red-hot. I have a plan.

> *Music. Several SAILORS take the post, as big as a battering ram, and sharpen it, then hold it up to the fire.*

ODYSSEUS (*softly*). All right, aim for the eye. On three. One. Two. Three!

> *They ram the hot spike into the eye of the CYCLOPS. Blood spurts out of the socket.*

> *The CYCLOPS screams and bellows and covers his eye with his hands.*

CYCLOPS. Ahhhh! What have you done to me? I can't see! Help!

> *He reaches out to grab them.*

ODYSSEUS. Pull back!

> *The SAILORS retreat to the back of the cave.*

CYCLOPS. Urrgh! Where are they?

> *The hands go behind the curtain. Sound of the CYCLOPS moving aside the boulder. Fade lights up as sunlight floods the cave.*

CYCLOPS. Friends! Help me!

> *The voice of a NEIGHBOR CYCLOPS replies.*

NEIGHBOR CYCLOPS. Who calls for us?

CYCLOPS. I, your brother, Polyphemus! Help me, they are hurting me!

NEIGHBOR CYCLOPS. Who is hurting you, Polyphemus?

CYCLOPS. Nohb Adi! No-body is hurting me!

NEIGHBOR CYCLOPS. If nobody is hurting you then what are you complaining about?

CYCLOPS. No, not Nobody… Nohb Adi!

NEIGHBOR CYCLOPS. You're out of your mind. Don't bother us again.

CYCLOPS. No! Come back!

> *The CYCLOPS roars with fury and begins flailing his arms in front of the entrance.*

CYCLOPS. You may have blinded me, but you'll still never get past me!

POLITES. How will we get out?

> *ODYSSEUS looks around frantically.*

ODYSSEUS. The sheep!

POLITES. Huh?

ODYSSEUS. The sheep!

ODYSSEUS takes a SHEEP and hoists it onto POLITES' back.

SAILORS. Ohhhhhh!

Other SAILORS all grab SHEEP, making the creatures ride "piggyback." They press past the CYCLOPS' hands and mouth, as the hands run over the backs of the SHEEP.

CYCLOPS. What's this? Oh, it's you, little Persephone. And who is this? Hestia? Go on, dear. Oh, and the ram wishes to go, too? So be it.

EURYLOCHUS (*noticing that there's no SHEEP left for ODYSSEUS*). But captain, what about you?

ODYSSEUS. Shhhh!

EURYLOCHUS goes through.

CYCLOPS. Yes. You too, Gaia. Run along and graze, my darling. I wouldn't want your wooly coats drenched with the blood of wicked men... You've nowhere to hide, humans. Even if I can't see you I can smell you.

ODYSSEUS. You pathetic fool! You've already lost them. They were hiding under your sheep!

CYCLOPS. What?

ODYSSEUS. They got away, you oaf. As will I, in a moment.

CYCLOPS. No! Cretan! Ingrate!

ODYSSEUS. But before I do, I think you should know the name of the mortal who outsmarted you. It's not Nohb Adi. It's Odysseus the Greek!

CYCLOPS. What? No! Nooooo!

ODYSSEUS runs and rolls right under the hands of the CYCLOPS.

CYCLOPS. Hear me, father! I am your son, Polyphemus. Never have I asked you for anything, but now I am begging you, Father, grant me this: that Odysseus may never reach home alive; or if he does, let his spirit first be crushed, his crew vanquished, his ship destroyed, his house filled with chaos. Curse him! Curse him! Curse him!

Music. Lights fade.

ACT 1, SCENE 4
"Shifting Winds"

Ithaca. PENELOPE watches the sea while YOUNG TELEMACHUS looks for shells in the sand.

Enter EURYCLEIA and TRAVELER.

EURYCLEIA. Mistress, here's the traveler you sent for.

PENELOPE. Telemachus, go play.

Exit YOUNG TELEMACHUS.

PENELOPE. You are a merchant?

TRAVELER. Yes, lady. For twenty years, I've sailed the wine-dark sea.

PENELOPE. And in all these travels, pray tell me, have you heard any news of my husband, King Odysseus?

TRAVELER. Oh yes, lady, I can tell you the heroic saga of the Trojan Horse! The walls of Troy were nigh impregnable... Her mighty gates—

PENELOPE. Yes, thank you, I've heard this story many times. I mean after, after the horse, after the sacking. What's become of him?

TRAVELER. That I cannot say. I know Agamemnon reached home safely... Nestor rules again at Pylos. I half expected to find Odysseus here when I arrived. Perhaps something dreadful has befallen him. Anything can happen out there: storms, shipwrecks, vengeful gods.

EURYCLEIA. That's enough, you! She didn't ask you to speculate.

PENELOPE (*scolding*). Eurycleia! Thank you, sailor. You may go.

TRAVELER. You are most welcome, lady.

Exit TRAVELER. PENELOPE turns away, crushed.

EURYCLEIA. Mistress, you—

PENELOPE. That will be all, Eurycleia. Inform me if more travelers arrive.

EURYCLEIA. Yes, Mistress.

Back on Isle of the CYCLOPS, The SAILORS rush to the ship, fleeing the CYCLOPS. Thunder sounds.

EURYLOCHUS. Row, sailors! Row! Smite the very sea with your oars!

ODYSSEUS. Looks like there's a storm coming.

ELPENOR. Captain! Giant waves out of nowhere.

ODYSSEUS. We'll meet them head on.

EURYLOCHUS. Brace for waves!

POLITES. Poor Antiphus! I miss him already.

PERMENIDES. The ship won't feel the same without him.

EURYLOCHUS. Brace!

MNESTHEUS. Not to mention we'll be short an oarsman.

ODYSSEUS. We should be short an oarsman, but we're not…

MINNOW. What's that you say, Captain?

EURYLOCHUS. Brace!

ELPENOR. He's right! We should be one fewer in number, but our number is the same!

SAILORS (*ad libbing*). "That's odd," "How can that be?" etc.

DOLIUS (*pointing at AEOLUS*). You! I've never seen you before.

AEOLUS. Nonsense. I've been here this whole time.

DOLIUS. No, you haven't. Who are you?

SAILORS (*ad libbing*). "Who is he?" "I don't know," "He should tell us who he is," etc.

EURYLOCHUS. Declare yourself.

AEOLUS. Oh, enough of this.

He waves his hand and all the men freeze except ODYSSEUS.

ODYSSEUS. My men!

AEOLUS. Sorry. They were being a nuisance. One moment.

He opens a leather bag and a giant suction sound is heard. The STORM and the WAVES disappear.

ODYSSEUS. The storm… You—

AEOLUS (*indicating the bag*). A handy piece of luggage, is it not?

ODYSSEUS. So you must be...

AEOLUS. Gods can appear in many shapes and sizes, Odysseus. You know this.

ODYSSEUS. I do, of course.

AEOLUS. Do you know why I want to help you?

ODYSSEUS. You want to help me?

AEOLUS. It's not because you're handsome. Your success at Troy was remarkable.

ODYSSEUS. Yes, I thank Zeus we were victorious.

AEOLUS. Oh, come! I am not talking about Zeus. That horse you invented! With one new idea, you accomplished in a day what fifty thousand men with swords couldn't do in ten years. A mortal who uses his mind should be supported, not punished. And believe me, Odysseus, you need more support now than even you can imagine.

ODYSSEUS. I do?

AEOLUS. Yes. Here, take the bag. (*tosses it*)

ODYSSEUS. So, this bag… it holds the storm from before?

AEOLUS. Oh no, it holds much more than that. All the winds in the world are in this bag. That's why it's so calm now, see? Don't tell my cousin Poseidon, but the seas are nothing without the wind. Oh, but how silly of me! I forgot to leave out the west wind. You'll need that to get home. Give it here.

ODYSSEUS tosses the bag back.

AEOLUS. Let's see if I can extract it for you.

AEOLUS opens the bag a tiny bit.

AEOLUS. Come on out, west wind, don't be shy! There, that's it.

The sound of the west wind returning to the air.

ODYSSEUS. Incredible!

AEOLUS. You should be home in nine days. Your men won't even have to row a stroke! But I suppose I'll unfreeze them anyway, as a courtesy to you.

ODYSSEUS. Thank you.

AEOLUS. Only remember: you mustn't open the bag until you reach Ithaca. That's very important.

ODYSSEUS. I promise I won't!

AEOLUS. Good man. Farewell, Odysseus!

Exit AEOLUS, on a summoned cloud.

SAILORS unfreeze.

MAKAR. The storm's gone!

EURYLOCHUS. And we're back on course…

POLITES. And where did that man go?

ODYSSEUS. That was Aeolus, Master of the Four Winds.

DOLIUS. He was a god? Oh no! I fear we were rude to him.

ODYSSEUS. Rest easy, Dolius. He favors us. And as his favor tends, so goes the wind. Now, onward, men. To Ithaca!

Ithaca. PENELOPE stands on the beach, still staring out at the sea.

EURYCLEIA. Mistress, your dinner is ready.

PENELOPE. Thank you, I'm not hungry.

EURYCLEIA. Why do you torture yourself, mistress? Staring at the sea, day after day.

PENELOPE. It is not by choice, Eurycleia, I assure you.

EURYCLEIA. What must it take to convince you that the master is gone?

PENELOPE. Much more than this. But you are right about one thing. I don't think I can bear to look at the sea any more today. Come.

Exit PENELOPE and EURYCLEIA.

Enter YOUNG TELEMACHUS.

YOUNG TELEMACHUS. Mother, look at the shell I found! Mother?

He looks out at the sea as the sound of the waves swells.

Back on the ship.

ELPENOR. I see them! The cliffs of Ithaca! Look there!

PERMENIDES. Can it really be? It feels like a dream.

MNETHEUS. But it is! I could draw those hills blindfolded.

MAKAR. Oh, what a sight for sore eyes!

EURYLOCHUS. This means we should make landfall in a few hours, Captain.

ODYSSEUS (*overwhelmed*). Aye…

EURYLOCHUS. Captain, you're exhausted!

ODYSSEUS. It's true. I haven't slept in a week. Too worried about reaching home.

MINNOW. Well, you should get some sleep now while you can, Captain.

MNESTHEUS. You won't want Penelope to see you like this.

MINNOW. Come on, Captain. Rest, and let the wind do the work.

ODYSSEUS thinks.

ODYSSEUS. All right.

MINNOW. That's the stuff, Captain!

ODYSSEUS. Eurylochus, you're in charge. Wake me if there's a problem.

EURYLOCHUS. Yes, Captain.

ODYSSEUS. Perhaps I'll get a pleasant dream for once.

> *Lights down on the ship. Enter YOUNG TELEMACHUS in spotlight.*
> *He gazes into the distance. His face lights up.*

YOUNG TELEMACHUS. A sail! A sail! Eumaeus, come quick!

EUMAEUS. What's that you say, Telemachus?

YOUNG TELEMACHUS. Eumaeus, look at the sail on that ship!

EUMAEUS. Why, that's an Ithacan sail! The same as the one on your father's ship. We must run and tell the mistress!

> *They exit. Lights up on the ship. EURYLOCHUS, DOLIUS, MINNOW,*
> *MNESTHEUS, ELPENOR, and POLITES drink wine as all the other*
> *men lie sleeping.*

> *They are just finishing up the last line of a drinking song.*

ALL.
For he who hath no pointed spear,
Nor leather shield, nor belted sword,
Will cower at my burly knee
And call me his master and his lord!

> *All cheer. EURYLOCHUS collapses with exhaustion.*

POLITES. Eurylochus!

ELPENOR. The poor clod could never hold his wine!

> *The SAILORS laugh.*

DOLIUS. Here's to home!

ALL. To home!

DOLIUS. And to Odysseus!

ALL. To Odyss—

MINNOW. I'm not toasting him.

DOLIUS. And why not?

MINNOW. Because he wouldn't toast you. Or me. Or any of us, even after all the years we've sailed with him. Odysseus thinks only of himself.

DOLIUS. Nonsense. He loves us. He sees us as equals.

MINNOW. If that's true, then why won't he tell us what's in the bag?

DOLIUS. What?

POLITES. Oh, you've been wondering about that, too?

MINNOW. Think about it. He hasn't opened it once, yet he never lets it out of his sight. It's treasure, I'll bet you anything.

ELPENOR. Oooh!

DOLIUS. So?

MNESTHEUS. So, remember when he wouldn't let us bring any spoils home from Troy? But now he gets to bring home his own treasure!

ELPENOR. I doubt he plans to share it with us.

MINNOW. Well, that's the whole idea, isn't it? We stay poor and he stays rich!

MNESTHEUS. I say we open the bag!

DOLIUS. But it isn't yours!

POLITES. We're not going to steal it, Dolius.

MINNOW. We just want to take a peek inside.

DOLIUS. Don't do it! Capta—

They cover his mouth.

MINNOW. Here goes…

MINNOW opens the bag. Instantly, a terrible storm arises. ODYSSEUS and the other SAILORS wake up.

MINNOW. Uh oh…

MAKAR AND MNESTHEUS. STORM!

ODYSSEUS. Fools! What have you done?

> *EURYLOCHUS and ODYSSEUS start shouting. MINNOW starts to fall overboard.*

PERMENIDES. Minnow, no!

MAKAR. Here, Minnow, take my hand!

ELPENOR. Look out!

> *Another gust of wind blows both MINNOW and MAKAR off the ship.*

ALL. Makar!

EURYLOCHUS. Here comes a wave! Hold on!

> *The ship is swept away to sea. SAILORS exit. Storm subsides.*

> *Back on shore. Enter YOUNG TELEMACHUS, PENELOPE, and EUMAEUS.*

YOUNG TELEMACHUS. But I saw them, Mother! Eumaeus saw them, too!

EUMAEUS. It's true, mistress. I could have sworn they were Ithacans.

PENELOPE. Whoever they were, they're gone now.

YOUNG TELEMACHUS. I really thought it was him this time.

PENELOPE. I know, Telemachus. You must learn to wait as I do. Hope is like a flame. Tend it patiently, or it will engulf you. Let's go inside.

> *Exeunt.*

ACT 1, SCENE 5

"Circe"

The sound of waves washing on the shore. The men have landed on a remote island. ODYSSEUS sits apart from the SAILORS, brooding.

POLITES. We're sorry, Captain. We didn't know.

ODYSSEUS. Don't talk to me.

 Pause.

DOLIUS. Captain, I know things look bleak, but we need orders.

ODYSSEUS (*indicating POLITES, ELPENOR, DOLIUS, MNESTHEUS*). Ask those four for orders. They seem to be leading the ship now.

EURYLOCHUS. Captain, Dolius defended you. He tried to stop them.

ODYSSEUS. Oh, did he? Was he the one I left in charge?

EURYLOCHUS. Captain, I'm sorry. I feel terrible. But don't you think someone should explore this island? See if there's food here? Captain?

ODYSSEUS. You can starve for all I care.

ELPENOR. Well, I'm going hunting!

MNESTHEUS. I'll come, too.

POLITES. And me!

EURYLOCHUS. I think I'll go with them, to keep an eye on them.

ODYSSEUS. You do that.

 The SAILORS exit. Set up for the house of Circe. The SAILORS re-enter.

POLITES. A house!

MNESTHEUS. Who would choose to put a house HERE?

 The sound of a woman's voice singing.

POLITES. Shhh! Listen. You hear that?

MNESTHEUS. A woman! Let's call to her!

EURYLOCHUS. Are you sure? She could be a witch.

POLITES. Hello!

>*The singing stops.*

POLITES. We are travelers in need of help. Can you tell us where we are?

>*CIRCE appears in the entryway. The SAILORS are awed by her beauty.*

CIRCE. Welcome, travelers. What a pleasure to have guests.

POLITES (*stammering*). The—the pleasure is ours.

CIRCE. I am Circe. I can see you've had a long, hard journey.

MNESTHEUS. We have.

CIRCE. Do you like cheese?

POLITES. Yes.

CIRCE. And what would you say to a bowl of barley meal, drizzled with sweet honey?

ELPENOR. We'd say that sounds wonderful!

CIRCE. Then you must come inside.

MNESTHEUS. We are honored!

>*They start to follow her.*

POLITES. Wait. Shouldn't we go tell the others first?

CIRCE. And did I mention there is wine?

POLITES. We can tell them later.

ELPENOR. In a few hours.

POLITES. Yes.

CIRCE. Come along, then, don't be shy.

>*POLITES and ELPENOR go in.*

MNESTHEUS. Eurylochus, won't you come with us?

EURYLOCHUS. I'd rather stay out here. Something about this place troubles me.

> *MNESTHEUS shrugs and goes inside. EURYLOCHUS finds a hiding place nearby. The three SAILORS sit down at the table. CIRCE and her SERVANT GIRLS serve them food.*

CIRCE. Here. Eat… and be refreshed!

> *They eagerly dig in.*

CIRCE. Good?

ELPENOR. Delicious!

CIRCE. Here, try the wine.

> *She squirts the wineskin into each SAILOR's mouth.*

SAILORS. Mmmmmm!

> *They return to eating.*

CIRCE. Now where did you sailors say you were from?

POLITES. Oh, we're from… we're from… Funny, I don't recall.

MNESTHEUS. Nor do I!

ELPENOR. I used to know, but now I don't!

> *They laugh, CIRCE the loudest.*

CIRCE. More?

MEN. Please!

CIRCE. Look at you brave, strong men! I can tell you just want to eat and eat and eat until your little bellies are full.

> *Their eating gets more and more messy and animal-like, with loud grunts and snorts.*

CIRCE. But be careful… because if brave strong men eat too much, they get SLOPPY. (*she taps ELPENOR with a stick and he falls behind the table*) They get GREEDY. (*she taps POLITES*) They get FAT. (*she taps MNESTHEUS*) And before you know it, they're no longer men. They're… PIGS!

> *The three SAILORS re-emerge from behind the table wearing pig snouts, snorting and grunting and scrambling on all fours.*

CIRCE. But are they good piggies or bad piggies? I think BAD!

> *She chases them around the room, swatting them with her stick.*

CIRCE. Yes, YOU'RE a bad piggy! And YOU'RE a bad piggy! And YOU'RE a bad piggy. Ha ha! You are bad, bad, naughty piggies!

> *POLITES looks at her angrily, trying desperately to speak, but all he can do is grunt.*

CIRCE. Don't grunt at me! I don't speak Piggish. Now shoo! To the sty with you!

> *She shoos them offstage, laughing. EURYLOCHUS emerges from his hiding place and runs offstage as the lights fade.*

> *Back at the ship, EURYLOCHUS arrives out of breath.*

PERMENIDES. Eurylochus, you're back!

DOLIUS. Did you find food?

EURYLOCHUS. O gods! O gods!

ODYSSEUS. What's the matter, Eurylochus?

EURYLOCHUS. Oh, Captain! It's awful! I mean, they were fine, they were themselves and then, poof! Transfigured! I wouldn't believe it except I saw it.

ODYSSEUS. Talk sense. What did you see?

EURYLOCHUS. She got 'em! She turned them all into pigs.

ODYSSEUS. Who changed who into pigs?

EURYLOCHUS. The witch. Circe. She lives in a house just over there. She invited us all in for some food. I told them it was a bad idea, but they wouldn't listen.

ODYSSEUS. You're lying.

EURYLOCHUS. I swear it's true!

ODYSSEUS. Wait here.

EURYLOCHUS. Oh, don't go, Odysseus! You'll be transfigured! Leave them behind.

ODYSSEUS. I'm not leaving them behind.

EURYLOCHUS. But they betrayed you! They're not worth it.

ODYSSEUS. Betrayers or no, they are my men.

> *ODYSSEUS takes his sword and starts his journey. PERMENIDES and DOLIUS exit, comforting EURYLOCHUS.*
>
> *Enter ATHENA.*

ATHENA. Hello, Odysseus.

ODYSSEUS. Are you the witch?

ATHENA. Look into my eyes and guess again.

> *ODYSSEUS looks and is taken aback.*

ODYSSEUS. Athena…

ATHENA. I assume many forms when I go among mortals—men, women, birds, beasts. But you can always tell it's me by my eyes.

ODYSSEUS. I'll remember that.

ATHENA. Your friend was right. Circe is sorceress of uncommon skill. If you face her without magic, you'll end up in the swine pen with the rest of your men.

ODYSSEUS. But I don't know any magic.

ATHENA. Here. Take this herb and put it under your tongue.

ODYSSEUS. Moly? But this is deadly poison!

ATHENA. Would I be giving it to you if it were poison? If you wish to keep your present shape, do as I say. Put the herb under your tongue, and when she offers you food, eat it. Drink the wine, too. And when she turns her wand against you, draw your sword and threaten her with it.

ODYSSEUS. Why?

ATHENA. Circe loves power. If she sees you as weak, she will dominate you. If she sees you as powerful, she will desire you. And desire unlocks many doors. Farewell, Odysseus.

> *She disappears. Reluctantly, ODYSSEUS puts the root under his tongue and approaches the house.*

ODYSSEUS. Who is there? Any welcome for a weary traveler?

> *CIRCE appears in the doorway and then beckons ODYSSEUS alluringly inside.*

ODYSSEUS. You're inviting me in?

> *CIRCE nods. She sits him down in a chair. She mixes her amnesia powder into a bowl and hands it to him. ODYSSEUS smiles and toasts her with the bowl, and CIRCE watches gleefully as he drinks every last drop.*

CIRCE. What's your name, traveler?

ODYSSEUS. Odysseus, of Ithaca.

CIRCE (*disappointed*). Oh. Are you sure?

ODYSSEUS. Quite sure.

CIRCE. That's odd.

ODYSSEUS. I don't see why.

CIRCE. Eat some more.

ODYSSEUS. With pleasure.

> *He eats some more, and she watches, annoyed. She taps him with her wand. It doesn't work.*

CIRCE. No. That's impossible. You're supposed to change into your true form.

ODYSSEUS. This is my true form.

CIRCE. No. You mortals are all the same on the inside; you're all bad piggies!

ODYSSEUS. You shouldn't generalize.

CIRCE. Don't tell me what to do. You're a BAD PIGGY. (*She taps him with her wand, but it doesn't work.*) Why won't it work?

> *ODYSSEUS draws his sword on her. CIRCE screams and falls to her knees, begging.*

CIRCE. What are you, a god? Why didn't the potion affect you?

ODYSSEUS. Where are my friends?

CIRCE. I will answer. But first, answer this. Do you think I'm beautiful? If you spare my life, I could be your lover and always be true to you.

ODYSSEUS. I don't need a lover, I need to see my friends. What have you done with them?

CIRCE. O please don't be angry, Odysseus! Spare me!

ODYSSEUS. I won't put my sword away until you swear by the gods not to harm anyone else.

CIRCE. I swear it! I swear.

ODYSSEUS. Good.

CIRCE. Girls!

> *SERVANT GIRLS enter.*

CIRCE. Prepare a feast for our visitor.

ODYSSEUS. What?

CIRCE. Only the best for him. Wine, nectar, pomegranates, anything he desires. And you, rub his shoulders.

ODYSSEUS. Hold on! I can't feast with you until my men are free. If you want to win me over, bring them here and undo your spell.

CIRCE (*reluctantly*). All right, fine!

> *She whistles and the three transformed SAILORS come trotting out as pigs.*

CIRCE. Roll over.

> *They each roll onto their bellies and by rubbing their bellies, she turns them back into men.*

POLITES. No more snouts!

ELPENOR. I'm me again!

MNESTHEUS. You look great.

ELPENOR. No, you look great.

ODYSSEUS. All of you stop it.

CIRCE. Now, brave Odysseus, bring the rest of your men here and I will prepare a great feast for you all. Music!

> *The SERVANT GIRLS begin to dance. The SAILORS stand amazed. ELPENOR whistles to summon DOLIUS, EURYLOCHUS, and PERMENIDES onstage. The SERVANT GIRLS flirtatously engage the SAILORS with dancing, grapes, and wine. They all pair off and exit in various directions.*

> *CIRCE takes ODYSSEUS by the hand and leads him offstage. Lights fade. Lights up. Enter CIRCE and ODYSSEUS.*

CIRCE. Another glorious morning! (*seeing his face*) What's wrong?

ODYSSEUS. Circe, I cannot thank you enough for the hospitality you have shown us. But it's been a month. It is time for me to leave.

CIRCE. I can't convince you to stay one more week? We've only just begun to know each other.

ODYSSEUS. I'm afraid not. My men are growing restless.

> *Two SERVANT GIRLS enter, leading MNESTHEUS and giggling. They are fitting him with a crown of flowers.*

MNESTHEUS (*excitedly, to ODYSSEUS*). They're making us all wear hats!

> *The SERVANT GIRLS pull MNESTHEUS offstage. CIRCE looks at ODYSSEUS skeptically.*

ODYSSEUS. Well, I grow restless. And you promised me that when the time came, you'd show me the way. Please. I miss my home.

CIRCE. Of course. I would not have you stay against your will. But when I said I knew the way, I may have… um… exaggerated.

ODYSSEUS. What?

CIRCE. Don't be upset! I can tell you how to find someone who knows.

ODYSSEUS. Who?

CIRCE. The Theban Prophet, Tiresias. He knows everything! The only problem is that he's...

ODYSSEUS. Dead.

CIRCE. Yes. To speak to him, you must travel to Hades.

ODYSSEUS. O gods! I can't go there!

CIRCE. But you must.

ODYSSEUS. No one has ever reached that place by ship, let alone returned from it.

CIRCE. That's because they didn't have my help.

> *CIRCE claps twice and two SERVANT GIRLS appear. One carries a ball of wax, the other a bowl filled with blood.*

CIRCE. Now listen well...

> *As CIRCE speaks, the lights change, and the SAILORS reassemble on the ship.*

ACT 1, SCENE 6

"To the Land of the Dead"

CIRCE. First you will meet the Sirens. Their songs are marvelous but deadly. Men who hear them will want to go on listening forever.

ODYSSEUS (*speaking to his men*). So if you ever wish to reach home, you must keep your ears plugged as you row.

MNESTHEUS. But Captain, how are we to be plug our ears and row at the same time?

ODYSSEUS (*producing a ball of wax*). With this!

SAILORS. Beeswax?

ODYSSEUS. Everyone, take a handful and stop up your ears on my command.

> The SAILORS each take a bit of beeswax.

PERMENIDES. And what about you, Captain? Will you stop your ears as well?

ODYSSEUS. No, Permenides. My curiosity forbids me. If all goes as planned, I'll be the first mortal to hear Siren-song and live to tell of it.

EURYLOCHUS. But Captain!

ODYSSEUS. Circe told me of a way to do it safely. Permenides, take this rope and tie me to the mast-block. Tie it tight, so I am bound fast. And once I am bound, remember this: no matter what I do or say, row on. I may order you, I may beg you to let me go. You are not to obey. Understood?

SAILORS. Aye, Captain.

ODYSSEUS. Now plug up your ears and start rowing.

> The SAILORS do as they are told. The SIRENS appear.

ODYSSEUS. I see one! Hold fast!

SIRENS (*singing*).
O I know a secret whispered by the stars
O I know the ageless wisdom of the trees
O I know a tale I carry from afar
You may hear it if you'll only come with me
You may hear it if you'll only come with me

O I know what ships do sail beyond the sky
O I know what lies beneath the wine-dark sea
O I know a meadow hidden from men's eyes
You may see it if you'll only come with me
You may see it if you'll only come with me
You may see it if you'll only come with me

> *The SIRENS continue to hum the melody as one of them addresses ODYSSEUS.*

SIREN. Come, Odysseus.

ODYSSEUS. You know of me?

SIREN. Of you. Of Troy, of all that was and all that will be on this bounteous earth. And we can share it all with you if only you'll come with us.

ODYSSEUS. I will! I mean, I want to, more than anything!

SIREN. Then take my hand.

ODYSSEUS. I… I cannot! Men, untie me! Undo the ropes! Sailors, listen to me. Everything I said before was wrong! I didn't understand anything until now. Everything is meaningless except the Siren-song! Stop rowing! Men, that's an order! Stop rowing, I beg you! Please, please Eurylochus! Untie the ropes! Permenides, look at me!

PERMENIDES. Hang on, Captain. Only a little farther and you'll be rid of them.

ODYSSEUS. I never want to be rid of them! I want to be rid of all of YOU!

> *Meanwhile, a SIREN reaching over the side of the ship attracts the attention of MNESTHEUS in the front row. Captivated by her beauty, he reaches out to touch her.*

EURYLOCHUS (*shouting deafly*). Just a little farther, captain. (*noticing*) Mnestheus, no!

> *As soon as the SIREN touches his hand, the creatures turn snarling and vicious. After an intense tug-of-war, the SAILORS manage to pull MNESTHEUS away from the SIRENS. At last, the SIRENS recede. They resume their eerie humming as they exit.*

ELPENOR. Oh, gods be praised!

As the SAILORS comfort a confused and shaken MNESTHEUS, CIRCE reappears to narrate. As she speaks, the SAILORS slowly disembark and start digging a hole for ODYSSEUS to pour blood into.

CIRCE. When you have passed the Sirens, travel to shore, and walk until inland you come to the place where the River of Tears meets the River of Flame. There dig a hole, and pour forth the blood of a lamb. Just a trickle— that's all you'll need to awaken the spirits. The rest is for the prophet.

ODYSSEUS takes the bowl and pours the blood. A masked EMISSARY from the Underworld appears and extends a hand.

ODYSSEUS. Who are you?

EMISSARY. Come.

ODYSSEUS looks at the hand, then back at his men.

DOLIUS. Captain, don't!

PERMENIDES. No one has ever come back from there alive!

ODYSSEUS. There's no turning back now. Stay here, and whatever you do, don't go near the river.

MNESTHEUS. But Captain!

ODYSSEUS. Eurylochus, if I'm not back before sundown, leave without me.

EURYLOCHUS. We would never!

ODYSSEUS. Don't argue with me. You must. Be brave, my friend…

EURYLOCHUS (*crying*). Odysseus!

The SAILORS embrace ODYSSEUS.

ODYSSEUS. There, there, boys. I don't plan on staying long.

ODYSSEUS takes the hand of the EMISSARY and the lights go out. Chanting and strange sounds. A procession of SPIRITS creep out to greet ODYSSEUS. Among them he recognizes the faces of the three crewmen who perished, ANTIPHUS, MAKAR, and MINNOW.

ODYSSEUS. Antiphus!

SAILORS. Hello, Captain.

ODYSSEUS. Makar, Minnow!

MAKAR AND MINNOW (*holding hands*). Hello, Captain.

ODYSSEUS. Makar, aren't you angry at Minnow for getting you killed?

MAKAR. Why should I be?

MINNOW. There are no grudges here, Captain.

ODYSSEUS. You mean you are all at peace here?

MAKAR. Oh, no. There is no peace, either.

  Enter ELPENOR as a ghost.

ODYSSEUS. Elpenor? What are you doing here?

ELPENOR (*shrugs*). I died.

ODYSSEUS. But I just said goodbye to you! You were alive.

ELPENOR. I know. I died right after you left.

ODYSSEUS. How?

ELPENOR. I fell in the River of Flame.

ODYSSEUS. I told you not to go near it!

ELPENOR. I know. But I was curious. I'd never seen a river of flame before.

ODYSSEUS. You must be sorry you did that.

ELPENOR. You'd think so, wouldn't you? But we don't feel much of anything here, besides thirst.

SPIRITS. Thirst!

MINNOW. Please, Captain. Give us just a little.

ODYSSEUS. A little of what?

ANTIPHUS. The blood!

ODYSSEUS. I can't.

MAKAR. But there's none to be had here.

ELPENOR. And when you're alive, you never know how good it tastes!

MINNOW. Come on, Captain, just a taste.

ODYSSEUS. No!

SPIRITS. A taste. A taste. A taste to quench our thirst!

> *They swirl around ODYSSEUS, trying to get a taste of the blood.*

ODYSSEUS. No! Let go! It's not for you; it's for Tiresias!

> *At hearing the name of the prophet, the SPIRITS back off, murmuring TIRESIAS' name.*

> *Enter TIRESIAS.*

TIRESIAS. Who stirs me from my sleep?

ODYSSEUS. I. Odysseus, son of Laertes.

TIRESIAS. Is that blood I smell?

ODYSSEUS. Yes. Take it. It's for you.

TIRESIAS. Ahh, yes. The living wine. (*he drinks*) Tell me, Odysseus, son of Laertes. Why have you left the light of day to visit me in this sad place?

ODYSSEUS. I have come to ask a question, great Tiresias. My men and I have been at sea for a year, on a journey that that was meant to last two weeks.

TIRESIAS. And what is your question?

ODYSSEUS. Will we ever reach home?

TIRESIAS. Oh, Odysseus. Why does it take a dead, blind man to show you what is right in front of you? You are cursed. Your men are cursed. Your ship is cursed.

ODYSSEUS. Why?

TIRESIAS. Because Poseidon holds a grudge against you.

ODYSSEUS. But that's impossible. I made sacrifices to Poseidon before our journey. I've done nothing to anger him.

TIRESIAS. Haven't you? Think back. Do you remember what you did to Polyphemus?

ODYSSEUS. Who?

TIRESIAS. The cyclops. The one-eyed beast you blinded and mocked. He was Poseidon's son.

ODYSSEUS. Him? But he scorned the gods! He called them weak.

TIRESIAS. How else would you expect a bastard son to speak? The cyclops may resent his father, but blood is a powerful thing. (*licking some blood off his finger*) Poseidon has sworn that as long as he rules the sea, you shall never reach home. He wants you destroyed.

ODYSSEUS. This is grave news indeed, Tiresias... But you still haven't answered my question.

TIRESIAS. Ha! True. Poseidon may have sworn it, but that doesn't make it certain. Yes, there is a chance you may reach home. But not without great hardship.

ODYSSEUS. Tell me.

TIRESIAS. Return to your ship, and follow the constellation of the hunter until you reach a rocky strait. It is a deadly place, but there is no way around it. Here you have two choices. If you pass along the left side, you will encounter Scylla. She dwells in the cliff wall, a vile, six-headed monster with an insatiable appetite for human flesh.

ODYSSEUS. And if I avoid her and go right?

TIRESIAS. Then you come within reach of Charybdis, a gargantuan creature that lurks below the surface. When she senses prey is near, she will open her gaping mouth and suck you down into her vortex.

ODYSSEUS. But is there no way to pass through the middle, and avoid both monsters?

TIRESIAS. Daredevil. No, you must choose. And if I were you, I'd choose the first. Better to lose a handful of men than your entire crew.

ODYSSEUS. Tiresias, who is that woman sitting there?

TIRESIAS. She is your mother.

ODYSSEUS. What? No... It can't be.

TIRESIAS. I tell no lies.

ODYSSEUS. But why does she not turn and look at me? Can she hear?

TIRESIAS. She is like most of the spirits here. She will not talk unless you give her blood. Now let me return to my sleep.

TIRESIAS exits.

ODYSSEUS offers his mother the blood. She drinks thirstily and hands the bowl back.

She looks up at him and her memory returns.

ANTICLEA. My son.

ODYSSEUS. Mother...

ANTICLEA. Odysseus! You're... alive. What are you doing here?

ODYSSEUS. I had to come here. I had to find the ghost of the Theban prophet to tell me how to reach Ithaca.

ANTICLEA. Have you been wandering all this time?

ODYSSEUS. I've had a few misfortunes.

ANTICLEA. My poor child.

ODYSSSEUS. Mother, it breaks my heart to see you here. How did you die? Were you sick?

ANTICLEA. I did not die of illness, but of longing. Longing for a cherished son to come home.

ODYSSEUS. I've been trying, Mother.

ANTICLEA. I know you have. None of us had any choice in this. I wanted to be with my son, and I couldn't. So I stopped living.

ODYSSEUS. But tell me, what news of Penelope? Does she still live?

ANTICLEA. She lives. She waits for you. Telemachus is growing more each day.

ODYSSEUS. Oh that is joyful news! Thank you, Mother—

He reaches out to her.

ANTICLEA (*recoiling*). Don't touch me!

ODYSSEUS. I only meant to comfort you.

ANTICLEA. You don't understand what it means to be dead. I may look the same, but there is no flesh, no bone, no sinews here. There is nothing holding me together.

ODYSSEUS. Mother, please!

ANTICLEA. Go home, Odysseus. Return to your son, and treasure every moment you have left with him. For once you come here, you'll see that we are remembered not by our deeds, but by the people we leave behind.

ODYSSEUS. Mother, I won't leave you.

ANTICLEA. Go! The longer you stay here, the harder it will be for you to leave.

 Exeunt.

ACT 1, SCENE 7
"Scylla and Charybdis"

Back on the ship.

EURYLOCHUS. Captain, look… An opening in the rock.

DOLIUS. So dark in there…

ODYSSEUS. That must be it. The Strait of Scylla. Now, remember my instructions. Keep to the left wall.

POLITES. Captain, what should we do if we see the monster?

ODYSSEUS. Pray.

> *They enter the strait. Lights dim. Silence. SAILORS nervously scan the rocky walls above.*

DOLIUS. I don't see anything…

MNESTHEUS. Perhaps she's not at home.

> *The SAILORS laugh nervously.*

> *Blackout.*

EURYLOCHUS. What happened? Where'd the light go?

> *SCYLLA sounds. DOLIUS screams as he is dragged offstage. Lights up.*

MNESTHEUS. What was that?

ODYSSEUS. Is everyone all right?

PERMENIDES. Dolius! Where's Dolius?

MNESTHEUS (*touching the deck*). There's blood here!

EURYLOCHUS. The thing must have got him!

ODYSSEUS. Everybody on your guard! Polites, get your spear.

> *Eerie, insect-like sounds of the creature moving along the rocks.*

PERMENIDES. Do you have a shot?

POLITES. I hear it, but I can't see it! (*seeing it*) Wait… There!

Blackout. Scylla sounds. POLITES screams as he is dragged offstage. SAILORS scream. Lights up.

ODYSSEUS. Polites! No!

PERMENIDES. He never even had a chance.

MNESTHEUS (*drawing his sword*). Well, I'm not going to die like that!

EURYLOCHUS. Mnetheus, what are you doing?

MNESTHEUS. Come on, you coward! Let's see how you like the taste of my blade.

ODYSSEUS. Mnestheus, don't!

Blackout. SCYLLA sounds. MNESTHEUS screams as he is dragged offstage. Lights up.

SAILORS scream.

EURYLOCHUS. O gods, o gods…

ODYSSEUS. Get this ship away from the wall!

PERMENIDES. But Captain, the Charybdis…

ODYSSEUS. If we stay this course, we'll all be dead in seconds. Man the oars.

They travel to the middle of the strait.

ODYSSEUS. If we stay to the middle, there's a chance she won't awaken…

EURYLOCHUS. Easy oars… Easy…

ODYSSEUS. Look out for that rock!

Thump.

EURYLOCHUS. Oh no…

A whirlpool begins to form. Music.

PERMENIDES. The sea is opening up!

ODYSSEUS. Hold on!

> *The WAVES get more violent, rocking the ship. PERMENIDES is thrown off.*

PERMENIDES. Help!

> *PERMENIDES is pulled under. The ship is torn apart. EURYLOCHUS and ODYSSEUS cling to one another.*

EURYLOCHUS. Captain!

ODYSSEUS. Hang on, dear friend! I can't lose you, too.

EURYLOCHUS. Odysseus, my hand is slipping!

> *Their grip is broken.*

ODYSSEUS. Eurylochus!

EURYLOCHUS. Odysseus!

> *EURYLOCHUS is pulled under.*

ODYSSEUS. No! No!

> *Fade to black.*

> *A voice hums a soothing melody in the darkness.*

> *ODYSSEUS wakes up with a start. His head is lying in a woman's lap, but he can't make out her features. She is stroking his hair.*

ODYSSEUS (*coughing*). Eurylochus! No! Eurylochus…

CALYPSO. Shhhh… Relax…

ODYSSEUS. Penelope?

CALYPSO. I thought I'd lost you.

ODYSSEUS. Penelope, where am I? Have I died, too?

CALYPSO. You were nearly dead. But now you're not.

ODYSSEUS. But the ship, I saw it smashed to pieces!

CALYPSO. Yes... I found you floating.

ODYSSEUS. My men. They're dead. I watched them die.

CALYPSO. Shhhh... Breathe... You're safe now.

ODYSSEUS. Penelope, where are we?

CALYPSO. Home.

ODYSSEUS. Home. Yes. And this is our bed...

CALYPSO. Yes. You are home now. And you never need leave here, ever again.

She kisses him.

ODYSSEUS. Penelope?

Lights go up.

CALYPSO. No. Calypso.

Blackout.

INTERMISSION

ACT 2, SCENE 1

"Suitors"

Ithaca, the palace. A group of SUITORS occupies the main hall. SERVANTS wait on them.

EURYMACHUS. So then I did what any man of good breeding would do. I punched him.

NOEMON. Liar! You never punched a centaur in your life.

EURYMACHUS. I swear to you it's true! Antinous, back me up.

ANTINOUS. It really happened. Just like the time he challenged Zeus to a game of backgammon.

EURYMACHUS. It was Zeus, I'm sure of it. And I won, three out of five!

NOEMON. Oh, shut up. Hey, more wine over here!

EURYCLEIA. Already? I just poured you some.

NOEMON. Yes, but see this? (*turning his cup upside down*) That's no good. That means "more wine needed."

She stares at him defiantly.

NOEMON. Well?

EURYCLEIA. I think the word you're looking for is "please."

NOEMON. Please. And one of those suckling pigs, if you've got it. You know, where the skin's all crackly and nice?

EURYCLEIA walks away in a huff.

ANTINOUS. You have to finesse these things, Noemon. You're the reason she keeps bringing out the bad wine, the stuff they give out to traders.

NOEMON. Eh, wine is wine.

ANTINOUS. You WOULD say that.

Enter PENELOPE.

EURYCLEIA (*to PENELOPE*). They're asking for more wine.

PENELOPE. Give it to them.

EURYCLEIA. I don't know how much more I can take of this.

PENELOPE. Patience, Eurycleia. Rude as they may be, they are guests in this house. The gods have rules about these things.

EURYCLEIA. Yes, my lady.

    Exit EURYCLEIA. Enter PHEMIOS, a young bard.

NOEMON (*to PHEMIOS*). You there, boy! Sing us a song.

PHEMIOS. What sort of song?

ANTINOUS. A song of Troy.

PHEMIOS (*sings*).
How many ships for Helen of Troy?
How many ships, how many ships?
How many trees were cut to their knees
To bring her back over the ocean?
How many lives for Helen of Troy?
How many lives, how many lives?
How many husbands and how many wives?
To bring her back over—

PENELOPE. Sing no more, Phemios, I beseech you. The drinking and the cursing I can tolerate, but sing no songs of Troy in this house. It pains me too much.

    PHEMIOS bows and exits.

ANTINOUS. Of course, lady. Eurymachus, why did you make the boy do that?

EURYMACHUS. It was your request!

ANTINOUS. I can think of a better song.
(*sings*) Pe-ne-lo-pe, would you mar-ry me?
Your beauty makes me weak inside.

EURYMACHUS (*joining in*).
I'll give you all that you desire
If you will only be my bride

NOEMON. Penelope, ignore these songbirds. What you want is a big man like me. Everyone is afraid to mess with me, which means I never have to fight. I just do what I please all day. And if you marry me, I'll let you do as you please. Live and let live, that's my motto.

EURYMACHUS. Ha! Drink and let drink, that's his motto.

PENELOPE. Gentlemen, please. There is very little you can give me that I don't already have.

ANTINOUS. I can think of a few things.

PENELOPE. If any of you think you can compare to Odysseus in my eyes, you are much mistaken.

ANTINOUS. We do not aim to compare ourselves with Odysseus in any way but one. We are alive, and Odysseus is dead. There, I said it.

EURYMACHUS. It needed to be said. After all, how long has it been since anyone has seen him? Ten years?

ANTINOUS. It is a fact we all must face, Penelope.

NOEMON. It grieves us all.

ANTINOUS. And I'm not saying I know how he died.

EURYMACHUS. Perhaps he drowned.

NOEMON. Perhaps he starved.

EURYMACHUS. Perhaps his brains were dashed out on a rock!

ANTINOUS. Boys, that's enough!

NOEMON & EURYMACHUS. Sorry.

ANTINOUS. What my friends mean, Penelope, is that as much as it pains us to admit it, Odysseus is dead, and it would be a terrible shame to watch beauty like yours simply wither on the vine. You must choose one of us to marry.

PENELOPE. Honestly, Antinous, I hear this speech from you so often I am beginning to wonder who it is you seek to persuade: me, or yourself. For my part, I long ago conceded the death of my husband. And as I have so often told you, I will be happy to marry one of you as soon as I have finished his burial shroud.

The SUITORS groan.

PENELOPE. Even if there is no body to cover, he must have a grave, and a fine shroud to cover it.

ANTINOUS. Forgive me, Penelope, but this is the same excuse you gave us two weeks ago!

EURYMACHUS. And the shroud hasn't gotten any longer!

PENELOPE. It is delicate work. And the more you pressure me to marry you, the more I am liable to make mistakes. And when I make a mistake, I have to unweave it and start again. You see?

SUITORS. Yes.

PENELOPE. You should all try a hand at weaving. It teaches patience.

NOEMON. Would it make you more likely to choose me?

PENELOPE. Doubtful.

NOEMON. Then I won't do it.

  Enter TELEMACHUS. He carries a short sword.

PENELOPE. Telemachus!

TELEMACHUS. Hello, Mother.

ANTINOUS. Why, if it isn't our young host!

EURYMACHUS. Hail to the boy-king!

NOEMON. Huzzah.

TELEMACHUS. I'd like to speak to my mother for a moment… alone.

EURYMACHUS. Chilly. I don't think he likes us.

NOEMON. Come on, lads, let's go see what's happening with that wine we asked for.

ANTINOUS. Careful with that sword. Your mother wouldn't want to see you get hurt.

  SUITORS exit, laughing.

PENELOPE. We haven't seen you in a few days.

TELEMACHUS. I've been up in the hills, training. With Eumaeus.

PENELOPE. You've been playing at swords with that old swineherd since you were nine.

TELEMACHUS. But it's not a game anymore, Mother. Eumaeus is teaching me to practice real combat.

PENELOPE. I'm glad, but I need you here. The house is in shambles, the servants are on edge, and every day it's more suitors at the door.

TELEMACHUS. Then let's throw them out!

PENELOPE. You know it's not that simple. By law they are guests in this house.

TELEMACHUS. Guests would have left a month ago. This is a siege!

PENELOPE. Keep your voice down. You think I don't know that? You think I don't wish every one of them dead?

TELEMACHUS. Then let me kill them for you.

PENELOPE. You? You're a child.

TELEMACHUS. I'm not! Look at me, Mother. I'm a man now.

PENELOPE. Yes… I suppose you are.

> *PENELOPE turns away in thought.*

TELEMACHUS. What is it?

PENELOPE. Nothing. I wish your father were here.

TELEMACHUS. So do I… Mother, I know you've started telling other people you've given up. But you haven't, have you?

PENELOPE. No. Not that I can explain why. It's just a feeling I have… that somewhere, somehow, your father is alive. Struggling, but alive, and determined to come back to us. I know it makes no sense. I've tried to make the feeling go away, but I can't. And as long as it remains, I will do everything I can to help him. Right now, that means buying him time, not fighting. You understand?

TELEMACHUS. Yes, Mother.

PENELOPE. Good. Don't take on the suitors by yourself. They'd rip you apart.

Enter EURYCLEIA.

EURYCLEIA. Mistress, there's another man at the door.

TELEMACHUS. Here they come, like pigs to slop.

PENELOPE. Telemachus will answer it.

EURYCLEIA nods and exits.

TELEMACHUS. I will?

PENELOPE. Yes. And you will show this man our warmest hospitality.

TELEMACHUS. Why?

PENELOPE. Because I know a few things about combat, too. Wait to strike, and in the meantime, never let your opponent see your anger.

TELEMACHUS (*sighs*). All right. I'll try.

Exit PENELOPE.

Enter ATHENA. Looking around the foyer, she turns her back to TELEMACHUS so he cannot see her face at first.

TELEMACHUS. Hail, stranger, you are welcome here! Would you care to dine with us?

ATHENA. That depends on what you're having. (*turning around*) I'm partial to ambrosia myself.

TELEMACHUS (*in wonderment*). You?

ATHENA. Hello, Telemachus.

TELEMACHUS. But… she said it was a man.

ATHENA. And to her eyes, it was.

TELEMACHUS. Well, you're a welcome sight to these eyes. Why have you come back?

ATHENA. Because it's time.

TELEMACHUS. Time for what?

Enter the SUITORS with SERVANT GIRLS waiting on them.

ANTINOUS. Now here's the sort of wine I was expecting from royalty.

EURYMACHUS. What do you say, Antinous? Another round?

ANTINOUS. Why not? More wine here, lass! (*noticing the server*) My, my, look at you. So lovely! Noemon, which of the servant girls do you prefer?

NOEMON. Who says I can't prefer them all?

ANTINOUS. Ha ha! Good lad!

EURYMACHUS. Speaking of beauties, who is that captivating creature there?

ANTINOUS. Indeed! Telemachus, aren't you going to introduce us to your pretty guest? I'm sure she'd like to meet a REAL man.

ATHENA turns away.

NOEMON. Ha! He's been spurned.

ANTINOUS. She likes me, she's just afraid to show it. A toast to the lady! (*He toasts, then screams as he brings the cup to his lips.*) Aaah! (*shaking it onto floor*) Get it away, get it off me!

NOEMON. Eww. What is it?

EURYMACHUS. I've never seen a spider that big!

NOEMON laughs.

ANTINOUS. What are you laughing at? You put it in my drink, didn't you!

NOEMON. No.

ANTINOUS. It's just the sort of thing you'd do.

NOEMON. I didn't do anything.

ANTINOUS. Don't lie to me. (*charging at him*) I'll kill you!

NOEMON. Hey, get off me! I didn't do it, I swear!

ANTINOUS chases NOEMON out. EURYMACHUS laughs, picks up the spider, and follows.

EURYMACHUS. Oh, Antinous, I have a present for you!

He exits.

TELEMACHUS. I apologize for that.

ATHENA. The situation here is even worse than I'd anticipated. Your father would be outraged to see his home defiled in this way.

TELEMACHUS. Are you telling me my father is alive?

ATHENA. Do you think he's alive?

TELEMACHUS. My mother still does. I have my doubts.

ATHENA. But you are a man now, or so I've heard. Why not find out for yourself?

TELEMACHUS. How would I do that?

ATHENA. Take a ship and go exploring. King Menelaus knew your father well, and he was the last of the Greeks to come home. Go talk to him.

TELEMACHUS. But Mother says I'm not allowed to sail.

ATHENA. Then perhaps you shouldn't tell her.

TELEMACHUS. Right. What do I do first?

ATHENA. You will need a crew. Men you can trust.

TELEMACHUS. Right... Phemios! Peisander!

Enter PHEMIOS and PEISANDER.

PHEMIOS. Master Telemachus?

PEISANDER. You called, master?

TELEMACHUS. Phemios, you used to sail on a merchant ship with your father, yes?

PHEMIOS. Yes.

TELEMACHUS. And Peisander, you tie good knots, I've seen you.

PEISANDER. Why, thank you, master! I didn't think you've noticed!

TELEMACHUS. I am planning a voyage to Sparta. I need a man to row with me and a man to work the sail. Will you come?

PHEMIOS. Of course, master. Anything!

EURYCLEIA (*entering*). Master Telemachus, what's this I hear about a voyage to Sparta?

TELEMACHUS. Eurycleia, I am taking these servants with me to the court of King Menelaus. I wish to learn what's happened to my father.

EURYCLEIA. But you cannot go! You are your mother's one happiness! If anything were to happen to you...

TELEMACHUS. Eurycleia, I have to do this or my mother will never find peace. Promise me you won't tell her.

EURYCLEIA (*thinks*). Very well. I promise. But you must be careful!

TELEMACHUS. We will. Thank you, Eurycleia.

EURYCLEIA. Come. I'll help you pack.

    Exeunt.

ACT 2, SCENE 2

"Calypso"

The island of Ogygia, where ODYSSEUS has been stranded for eight years, with the nymph CALYPSO as his host. He sits by the water's edge, gazing out at the sea.

Enter CALYPSO.

CALYPSO. Why so solemn, love? Here, look what I brought. A crown, see? Just like Lord Apollo wears. Now you can be Lord Odysseus of the island.

ODYSSEUS ignores her.

CALYPSO. I've made you so many pretty things, yet all you care to look at is the sea.

ODYSSEUS. I'm not looking at it. I'm thinking about what's across it.

CALYPSO. What does it matter what's across it? You are here, now, beneath the stars with your Calypso. (*turing his head to her*) And look. She is beautiful.

ODYSSEUS. She is.

CALYPSO. And kind.

ODYSSEUS. Very.

CALYPSO. And immortal.

ODYSSEUS. True.

CALYPSO. And she is all you need.

ODYSSEUS. She is not all I need and you know that. I have a wife and a son waiting for me in Ithaca.

CALYPSO. Ithaca! Always Ithaca! I wish I could show you your Ithaca right now, and you would see what a dull place it is.

ODYSSEUS. Home doesn't need to be exciting.

CALYPSO. Or what if it's gone entirely? What if you come back to find your Ithaca burned as Troy was? It's possible. Outside here, nothing is for certain. So why risk more heartache when you can stay with me? My heart beats forever. And yours could, too, if you desire it to. Yes, I could make you immortal, Odysseus. You need only say the word. Think of it: never having to grow old. We could always be perfect, just as we are now.

ODYSSEUS. I don't want to be immortal.

CALYPSO. You don't?

ODYSSEUS. No. I want to be dead.

CALYPSO. You don't mean that.

ODYSSEUS. I do. I wish I'd died at Troy like a real warrior. But if you cannot give me death, then give me peace.

> *ODYSSEUS exits.*

CALYPSO. Yes, my love.

> *CALYPSO stares dejectedly out at the stars. ATHENA appears behind her.*

CALYPSO. I know you're there.

ATHENA. I wasn't hiding. I was observing your technique.

CALYPSO. Of course.

ATHENA. How long do you intend to keep playing house here, with a grown man as your doll?

CALYPSO. What is your message, Athena?

ATHENA. Zeus has spoken. He says Odysseus has suffered enough. It is time for the soldier to return home.

CALYPSO. No.

ATHENA. You cannot refuse.

CALYPSO. I do refuse.

ATHENA. You defy the will of Zeus?

CALYPSO. Why should Zeus care? We're happy here alone.

ATHENA. Maybe you are.

CALYPSO. Odysseus loves me. You don't know him as I do.

ATHENA. Perhaps. But your arrangement here is unbecoming of a goddess.

CALYPSO. Oh, now I see…

ATHENA. What?

CALYPSO. Zeus may philander about the world as he pleases, but he can't bear the thought that a goddess might choose a mortal husband!

ATHENA. This is not all Zeus's doing. In fact, it was I who convinced him.

CALYPSO. You?

ATHENA. I have been watching Odysseus for some time. I admire the man.

CALYPSO. DO you?

ATHENA. Yes. But not in the way that you do. It is rare to find a mortal so clever, so resilient. And it pains me to see him sitting on the beach day after day. He must return to his rightful place in Ithaca.

CALYPSO. Even if I let him go, he'll never survive. Poseidon—

ATHENA. Poseidon is on the other side of the world right now, distracted. Now is the perfect time to set sail.

CALYPSO. He has no ship.

ATHENA. Give Odysseus an axe, and he'll have a raft built in half a day. I know he's asked you for one in the past.

CALYPSO. You can't take him from me! He is only alive because I saved him. His ship was wrecked. He had nothing. I took him into my cave, fed him, clothed him, cared for him, loved him with all my heart.

ATHENA. Yes, Calypso. Now find it in your heart to release him.

CALYPSO retrieves a small bronze hatchet from a hiding spot on stage.

CALYPSO (*calling out*). Odysseus!

Enter ODYSSEUS.

ODYSSEUS. What now?

CALYPSO (*holding out the hatchet*). I have a gift for you. Use any tree you like to make your raft. Leave tonight. Follow the stars, and keep the constellation of Orion on your left to reach Ithaca.

ODYSSEUS (*amazed*). Thank you.

He kisses her and then exits.

CALYPSO (*looking out at the stars*). And remember me...

Lights fade.

ACT 2, SCENE 3
"Where Is Telemachus?"

Ithaca, the palace. The SUITORS, still growing in number, sit around chatting and drinking. PENELOPE is pacing as EURYCLEIA watches, her face full of guilt.

Enter PHOEBE.

PENELOPE. Well? Was he there?

PHOEBE. No, Mistress. The swineherd says he hasn't seen Master Telemachus in four days.

PENELOPE. I was sure he'd be there. And Eurycleia, you looked along the beach?

EURYCLEIA. Along the... Oh, yes. Yes, Mistress.

PENELOPE. It doesn't make sense. Antinous, I know I've asked you this already—

ANTINOUS. I am sorry, Penelope. Your son's absence is as much a mystery to me as it is to you. All I can offer is my comfort—

PENELOPE (*shouting over SUITORS*). HAVE ANY OF YOU SEEN TELEMACHUS?

The SUITORS go quiet.

THOAS. Who?

NOEMON. Her son. He disappeared before you got here.

THOAS. Ohhh...

NOEMON. We haven't seen him.

PENELOPE. Phoebe, go into the village and ask around.

PHOEBE. Yes, Mistress.

ANTINOUS. Are you sure that's wise, Penelope?

PENELOPE. What do you mean?

ANTINOUS. Well, we don't know how the news is going to affect the public.

PENELOPE. My son is missing. I need to find him.

ANTINOUS. Of course. And you're worried about him; I understand that. But consider how it will look to your people. First they lost their king, and now the sole heir to the throne is missing. What will be their reaction?

EURYMACHUS. Panic?

ANTINOUS. Almost certainly.

NOEMON. And if the other kingdoms found out, they might invade.

ANTINOUS. Very possible. But there's a way to prevent all that.

PENELOPE. What?

ANTINOUS. Choose a husband now, today, and keep the line intact.

PENELOPE. Of course you bring it back to that. How dare you talk about succession at a time like this?

ANTINOUS. If not now, then when? You're always deferring, Penelope. First it was, "I'm finishing my burial shroud."

PENELOPE. I am! I'm still weaving it.

ANTINOUS. Nonsense. Eurymachus here saw you unweaving it last night.

PENELOPE. You were spying on me in my sanctuary?

EURYMACHUS. Only because I thought you were up to something! And you were!

ANTINOUS. Then it was, "Wait until Telemachus is a man."

LEOCRITUS. Well, now he's gone.

ANTINOUS. And you must choose.

LEOCRITUS. Marry one of us, and this will all be over.

NOEMON. You'll have your home to yourself again, and a husband to keep your bed warm.

ANTINOUS. Now, Penelope. Not another day should go by without a king on the throne of Ithaca…

BIAS. We'll accept your decision, whoever you pick.

THOAS. You just have to choose.

> *All the SUITORS start chanting "choose" at PENELEOPE as they close in around her.*

PENELOPE. I—

EURYCLEIA. Stop! Telemachus wasn't killed. He's alive. I know it for a fact.

PENELOPE. What? Where is he?

EURYCLEIA. Sparta. He took a ship, to find out what happened to master Odysseus.

PENELOPE. Eurycleia, why didn't you tell me before?

EURYCLEIA. I promised him I would keep it a secret.

PENELOPE. Come. Tell me everything.

> *Exit PENELOPE and EURYCLEIA. The SUITORS sigh and groan.*

EURYMACHUS. She was this close to choosing me!

BIAS. She was not!

EURYMACHUS. She was!

BIAS. Then why was she looking right at me?

NOEMON. You're both wrong. Did you see her lips? She was starting to say my name, "Nooo-emon."

> *The SUITORS shout him down and start bickering.*

ANTINOUS. Oh, shut up, all of you! (*They go quiet.*) Don't you see? She's never going to make a decision while the boy is alive. She'll just string us along for two more years until he comes of age. And then none of us will get the riches.

ELATUS. Or what if the boy comes back with news that Odysseus IS alive?

ANTINOUS. The thought gives me shivers. We can't let it happen.

EURYMACHUS. So, what do you propose, Antinous?

ANTINOUS. If we tried anything here, we'd get caught. But right now, the boy is at sea.

THOAS. Ah… There are all sorts of accidents that could befall a first-time sailor.

ANTINOUS. Exactly. So let's make sure one does…

POLYBUS. Anybody know a good spot?

BIAS. Halfway between Sparta and Ithaca there's a small island called Asteris. Any ship returning from Sparta is sure to stop there.

EURYMACHUS. Perfect. Who should go?

ANTINOUS. We'll draw straws…

Exit.

ACT 2, SCENE 4

"The Raft"

ODYSSEUS nods off on his raft. He awakes to find a wall of WAVES encircling him. They speak for the sea god, POSEIDON.

WAVES. ODYSSEUS…

ODYSSEUS. Poseidon!

WAVES. WHAT ARE YOU DOING ON MY SEAS?

A WAVE crashes over his ship.

ODYSSEUS. Let me go!

WAVES. YOU ARE TRESAPASSING.

Another WAVE crashes. ODYSSEUS struggles to keep the raft afloat.

ODYSSEUS. I wish you no ill, Poseidon.

WAVES. DID YOU THINK I WOULDN'T NOTICE?

ODYSSEUS. Let me be!

WAVES. DID YOU THINK YOU COULD FOOL ME LIKE YOU FOOLED EVERYONE ELSE?

ODYSSEUS. No! I just want to go home!

WAVES. HOME? YOUR HOME IS IN THE DEEP!

ODYSSEUS. Nooo!

The WAVES destroy the raft. ODYSSEUS clings to a piece of the mast. Attacked again and again by the storm, he is eventually pulled underwater. Sound of storm turns to the muffled quiet of being underwater.

ODYSSEUS is about to drown when INO, the sea nymph, swims up to him.

INO. Hello, Odysseus. I've been watching you from underneath the waves. Oh, don't be afraid. I'm not a monster. I am Ino, the sea nymph. But I was once a mere mortal like you! *(offering her scarf)* Here, you can breathe into this.

He takes it and breathes.

INO. It lets you speak underwater, too.

ODYSSEUS. Thank you!

INO. I see Poseidon is giving you a lot of trouble. But he hasn't managed to kill you yet, so that's something. Take my advice: abandon your craft and try to swim to shore. It is not far off.

ODYSSEUS. But I'll drown!

INO. Not if you wrap that scarf around your waist. That's right, you can borrow it. But as soon as your hand touches the shore, you must send it back. Promise?

ODYSSEUS. I promise. But how?

INO. Just throw it over your shoulder into the sea! I'll be there to catch it.

ODYSSEUS. You will?

INO. Oh, yes. I'm never far away…

> *ODYSSEUS swims to the surface, and another WAVE washes over him.*

ACT 2, SCENE 5

"Ambush"

The island of Asteris. TELEMACHUS and his crew have just made landfall.

PHEMIOS. This is the island I told you about, master. There's a spring just over that rise.

TELEMACHUS is lost in thought.

PHEMIOS. Master?

TELEMACHUS. Right. You two get a fire going. I'll go fetch the water.

PEISANDER. Master, wait. May I ask you something? You've barely said a word since Sparta. Did you... learn anything? From King Menelaus?

TELEMACHUS. I did. Forgive me for being taciturn, I just don't know what to make of what Menelaus told me. He said that in his travels, he met Proteus, a shape shifter who sees all that goes on across the wine-dark sea. The king asked him about my father. He said, "Odysseus is alive."

PHEMIOS. He is? That's wonderful!

TELEMACHUS. He's stranded, held captive on a faraway island, with no ship, and no crew.

PEISANDER. We'll sail there and rescue him!

TELEMACHUS. The island where he is held does not appear on any map. It is invisible.

PHEMIOS. At least he's alive.

TELEMACHUS. That brings me little comfort. In the end, I am happier to have seen a bit of the world with you than I am about that news. Just having sailed made me feel closer to him. As if he were in my blood.

PEISANDER. He is.

TELEMACHUS. Yes... Well, I'll go find that spring.

He exits. PHEMIOS and PEISANDER begin building a fire. Four SUITORS (including POLYBUS and EURYMACHUS) sneak up behind and murder them.

EURYMACHUS. Good. Now we wait for the prince to come back…

   SUITORS return to their hiding place. TELEMACHUS returns.

   Enter ATHENA.

ATHENA. Don't go this way.

TELEMACHUS. Why?

ATHENA. Your men are dead.

TELEMACHUS. What? No! I just left them.

ATHENA. The suitors set an ambush. They want you dead. You must find another way off this island. Go!

   Exit TELEMACHUS.

EURYMACHUS. He's trying to run. Polybus, after him!

POLYBUS. Why run? He's got no place to go.

EURYMACHUS. You fool! Our boat is docked over there.

POLYBUS. Uh oh.

EURYMACHUS. Run!

   Exit.

ACT 2, SCENE 6

"Disguises"

The sound of gentle waves and seagulls. ODYSSEUS wakes up alone on a beach.

ODYSSEUS. White sand... Poplars... Can it be?

SHEPHERD (*appearing behind him*). Greetings, stranger!

ODYSSEUS. Greetings, young shepherd. Tell me, what land is this?

SHEPHERD. You must be simple, stranger, or else very lost. This land is well known as far as distant Troy. A rugged land, where the people are hardy but kind, the grain grows wild, and the wine is sweet. You are in Ithaca.

ODYSSEUS (*delighted*). Ithaca! (*catching himself*) Ah, yes. Ithaca. I've heard it mentioned once, in the place where I am from.

SHEPHERD. And where is that?

ODYSSEUS. Crete.

SHEPHERD. Oh?

ODYSSEUS. Yes. Well, Lowland Crete, to be precise. My comrades and I arrived last night. We were sailing for Pylos, but a storm blew us off course.

SHEPHERD. That's odd. The seas have been calm all morning.

ODYSSEUS. Well, it was an early morning storm. You probably weren't up yet.

SHEPHERD. That must be it. Well, if you'd like, I can show you the way to the village.

ODYSSEUS. Yes, thank you.

SHEPHERD (*stepping out of view*). It's just on the other side of these trees.

ODYSSEUS. Are you sure? (*pointing in opposite direction*) I have a feeling the village is THAT way.

SHEPHERD (*out of view*). You're right. It is the other way. But how do you know that if you've never been here before?

ODYSSEUS. I—well, I...

    ATHENA appears, laughing.

ATHENA. Well? Where's that quick wit now?

ODYSSEUS (*kneeling*). Athena! That was you?

ATHENA. Of course it was. And you should have recognized me!

ODYSSEUS. The eyes...

ATHENA. Yes.

ODYSSEUS. I said I would remember, but I forgot.

ATHENA. And why were you lying to the little shepherd boy? Was he really such a threat?

ODYSSEUS. I don't know, one can never be too cautious.

ATHENA. Even when one is king?

ODYSSEUS. Especially when one is king.

ATHENA. Well, it turns out you were right to be cautious. Ithaca is not as you left it. Your home is overrun by wicked men. They seek to steal your wife and kill your son, and they will kill you if they get the chance.

    Pause. ODYSSEUS turns away from ATHENA and absorbs the news.

ODYSSEUS. How many of these men are in my house?

ATHENA. At least fifty. But more arrive each day.

ODYSSEUS. Too many for me to fight alone.

ATHENA. Yes. So for now, you'll have to lay low.

ODYSSEUS. How can I do that? I'm known here. (*realizing what she's planning*) Ohhh, no.

ATHENA. You need it.

ODYSSEUS. No. You are not turning me into the old man again.

ATHENA. It helped you once in Troy. Remember?

ODYSSEUS. But it's so uncomfortable!

ATHENA. Come now. It's only for a short while. Their loyalty must be tested.

ODYSSEUS. Oh, all right...

> *ODYSSEUS and ATHENA exit together.*
>
> *Set changes to the swine farm. EUMAEUS sits in his hut, making stew over a fire. Sound of dogs barking. EUMAEUS leaves his hut, stands near the entrance, and shouts at the offstage dog.*

EUMAEUS. Down, boy! Down! Stay... Come here, friend, come along. Don't be afraid. Sorry about that. He barks at all strangers.

> *Enter ODYSSEUS, disguised as an old beggar.*

ODYSSEUS. He's right to bark. I was trespassing.

EUMAEUS. An easy thing to do on a small island like this. What brings you here?

ODYSSEUS. A grave misfortune. My ship crashed on the rocks. I had to swim to shore.

EUMAEUS. Poor fellow! You must be tired and hungry. Come inside.

ODYSSEUS. It's awfully kind of you to invite me when I haven't even told you my name.

EUMAEUS. I don't need to know your name. I know who you are.

ODYSSEUS (*amazed*). You do?

EUMAEUS. You're like me! An old working sod with a sunburned face and hands like leather. You've had a rough life and not a lot to show for it. Right?

ODYSSEUS. Right.

EUMAEUS. Now, come. Have a seat by the fire.

ODYSSEUS. But isn't that your seat?

EUMAEUS. Zeus says that guests come first. And here in Ithaca, we obey the word of Zeus. To a fault, I should say. Here, have some stew.

ODYSSEUS. Thank you.

EUMAEUS. Don't get too excited. I only get to use the runty pigs. The fat ones go to the suitors.

ODYSSEUS. Suitors?

EUMAEUS. At the palace. Now that my master is dead, they sit there all day guzzling his wine and gorging themselves, all in the name of courting the widow. Disgraceful!

ODYSSEUS. How did your master die?

EUMAEUS. No one knows. He left for Troy years ago and never came back. Gods, I miss him! He was just a young man when he left, but already a great king. Wise, generous...

ODYSSEUS. What was his name? I fought at Troy, too. Perhaps I could give you news of him.

EUMAEUS. Oh, no! Forgive me, but if I have to hear one more traveler tell me of the Trojan Horse, I'll go mad.

ODYSSEUS. Then I could tell you of his journey home.

EUMAEUS. That would be a lie, then. Look, stranger, I'd be happy to hear of your adventures, but please, no tales about Odysseus.

Enter TELEMACHUS.

ODYSSEUS. A friend of yours is coming.

EUMAEUS. How do you know?

ODYSSEUS. I hear footsteps, but no barking.

TELEMACHUS (*entering*). Eumaeus! Eumaeus!

EUMAEUS. Telemachus! You're home!

TELEMACHUS. And very glad to be.

EUMAEUS. Oh, you are dearer to me than sunlight. I said to myself over and over, "Accept it, Eumaeus, the boy's never coming back." That's what I told myself so I wouldn't get my hopes up. But secretly I did have my hopes up!

TELEMACHUS. How is my mother? She hasn't married one of those suitors, has she?

EUMAEUS. No, but she's at her wit's end. We can talk of sad things later. Come in, have some stew.

TELEMACHUS (*noticing ODYSSEUS*). Eumaeus—

EUMAEUS. Or don't have stew. Whichever you like. Oh, it cheers my heart just to look at you. You must tell me all about your journey.

TELEMACHUS. Eumaeus!

EUMAEUS. What?

TELEMACHUS. Who's the old man?

EUMAEUS. Oh, my guest! Why, he's a shipwrecked traveler. Yes, come from...

ODYSSEUS. Lowland Crete.

EUMAEUS. Lowland Crete.

TELEMACHUS. Pleasure to meet you, stranger.

ODYSSEUS. The pleasure is mine. Please, have my seat.

TELEMACHUS. Oh, no, don't get up. If you are his guest, you are my guest.

ODYSSEUS. You are kind hosts here.

TELEMACHUS. This is nothing. Normally I'd invite you to stay at the palace, but I fear you'd meet a cold reception if we went there now.

ODYSSEUS. So I've heard.

TELEMACHUS. The suitors have no respect for anyone, not even my mother. And you, why if you walked in there, dressed as you are, and asked for food, I'd hate to think what they'd do. No offense.

ODYSSEUS. Oh, none taken.

TELEMACHUS. Eumaeus, go to the palace and tell my mother I'm home. Be sure no one else hears you.

EUMAEUS. Of course.

Exit EUMAEUS.

ODYSSEUS. So... you had an adventure, then?

TELEMACHUS. Adventure makes it sound thrilling. And I suppose it was, at first. Then I lost my friends, and it became more like a nightmare.

ODYSSEUS. Yes. I know the feeling.

Enter ATHENA. She transforms ODYSSEUS to his true form while TELEMACHUS has his back turned. ATHENA exits.

TELEMACHUS. I'd thought the journey would make me stronger. But it's only made it clear to me how vulnerable I am. How vulnerable we all are.

ODYSSEUS. That's called wisdom.

TELEMACHUS. I doubt my father would say so.

ODYSSEUS. No. He would. Telemachus, look at me.

TELEMACHUS turns around and is amazed.

TELEMACHUS. Who are you? What happened to you?

ODYSSEUS. Telemachus...

TELEMACHUS. Are you a god?

ODYSSEUS. I'm your father.

TELEMACHUS. No! They told me he was never coming back.

ODYSSEUS. Will you believe their words or your own eyes?

TELEMACHUS. It's a trick.

ODYSSEUS. It's no trick. The gods have brought me to you.

TELEMACHUS. I don't believe you!

ODYSSEUS (*slowly*). Telemachus, look at me. When you were a baby, I held you in these hands.

Pause. TELEMACHUS looks in his father's eyes, then at his hands.

TELEMACHUS. Father…

ODYSSEUS. Telemachus!

They embrace. Enter EUMAEUS.

EUMAEUS. Master Telemachus, I'm back! Your mother said to—what's all this?

ODYSSEUS. Hello, Eumaeus.

EUMAEUS (*shocked*). No. I'm dreaming.

ODYSSEUS. You're awake. I'm real. See? (*puts EUMAEUS' hand to his face*)

EUMAEUS. Master, is it really you?

ODYSSEUS. I've missed my swineherd.

EUMAEUS. Master! But how? The old man…

ODYSSEUS. A disguise. I'm sorry, old friend. I needed to see if you still believed in me.

EUMAEUS. But of course I did!

TELEMACHUS. Eumaeus was one of the few.

ODYSSEUS. That's all right. He's all we need.

TELEMACHUS. All we need for what?

EUMAEUS. Why, to take on the suitors, my boy!

TELEMACHUS. How do you mean? The three of us, against all those suitors?

ODYSSEUS. Don't worry, son. I have a plan.

They gather in a huddle. Lights fade.

ACT 2, SCENE 7
"Homecoming"

The courtyard of the palace. The SUITORS number more than ever before. ANTINOUS interrogates the four members of the ambush party.

ANTINOUS. He stole your boat?

EURYMACHUS. Yes, but then we stole his boat!

ANTINOUS. Oh, well, why didn't you say so? That changes everything.

NOEMON. It does?

ANTINOUS. No! Telemachus lives! And worst of all, he knows our game.

THOAS. Oh no! He'll tell Penelope what we've done...

POLYBUS. And that will make her even colder to us.

BIAS. She'll turn the people against us!

ANTINOUS. Right. So we have to act quickly.

ELATUS. How?

ANTINOUS. Any moment now Telemachus will be walking through those gates. No doubt he'll be furious at us for trying to kill him. So we must take advantage of that anger before he reaches Penelope. Rile him up. Get him to strike one of us. Then, if we kill him...

EURYMACHUS. It will be in self-defense!

ANTINOUS. Precisely. I'll do the honors.

NOEMON. Oh, no! Let me do it. I've been aching to skewer that little shrimp for a long time.

ANTINOUS. Fine, Noemon, you do it. But you must let him strike first.

NOEMON. I know, I know.

POLYBUS. There's someone at the gate!

ANTINOUS. Get ready, boys.

The SUITORS all stare at the gate in anticipation. The doors open. Enter the SOOTHSAYER.

SOOTHSAYER. Repent!

The SUITORS groan.

NOEMON. Oh, it's only the soothsayer!

SOOTHSAYER. I saw it! A sign from the heavens. I saw two eagles flying high above my shrine.

BIAS. You saw some birds. So what?

SOOTHSAYER. At first they flew side by side as brothers. Then all at once they turned on one another, slashing into each other with their talons, screeching and clawing and tearing away feathers.

BIAS. And?

SOOTHSAYER. It is a sign of dreadful things to come!

ANTINOUS. Get her out of here!

SOOTHSAYER. Make your peace with the gods! Repent! Repent!

The SUITORS push the SOOTHSAYER out the door.

ANTINOUS. All right. That was a bit of a false start. The next person who comes through those gates should be Telemachus.

POLYBUS. Someone else is coming!

The men watch the gates. The doors open. Enter EUMAEUS.

EURYMACHUS. It's that stupid old swineherd!

NOEMON. Swineherd, did you bring us any more suckling pigs?

EUMAEUS. No roast today. Only a friend, who needs your help.

EUMAEUS steps aside. The SUITORS wait in anticipation. Enter ODYSSEUS, disguised once more as a beggar.

SUITORS. Awww!

LEOCRITUS. A beggar? What did you bring him for?

ODYSSEUS. Please, gentles. A crust of bread or a scrap of meat for an old man in need?

THOAS. Eumaeus, I thought you said you didn't bring a swine.

ANTINOUS. Take your groveling elsewhere, baggage.

ODYSSEUS. Surely one of you will give me something!

MELANTHUS. Sure, I'll give you something!

ODYSSEUS. You will?

He kicks ODYSSEUS. The SUITORS laugh.

EUMAEUS. Leave him alone!

ODYSSEUS. It's all right, Eumaeus. Perhaps these men don't understand. You see, I was once a nobleman like you. And back then, I never denied a meal to any man that needed it. Because I knew that someday my fortunes might turn. And so they did. See? And someday your fortunes might turn, and you'll have to go begging. Be kind and generous while you can, because the gods are fickle, and we only have each other.

POLYBUS. He's preaching to us.

NOEMON. I say we practice on him.

SUITORS agree. They start shoving ODYSSEUS around, jeering, kicking him.

EUMAEUS. Stop it! Leave him alone!

Enter PENELOPE.

PENELOPE. Stop this at once! What on earth is going on here?

EURYMACHUS. It's not what it looks like.

ANTINOUS. We were only having a bit of fun with him.

PENELOPE. You. Come here. Are you hurt?

ODYSSEUS. A scratch, lady. Nothing I haven't dealt with before.

PENELOPE. Come inside. Eurycleia, tend to him.

EURYCLEIA. Yes, Mistress.

Exit EURYCLEIA and ODYSSEUS.

PENELOPE (*to SUITORS*). So, is that what I'm to expect if one of you becomes my husband? Beating up beggars for sport?

NOEMON. Now, to be fair, he struck first.

Enter TELEMACHUS.

PENELOPE. I don't want to hear it. And if you think that—

TELEMACHUS. Hello, Mother.

PENELOPE. Telemachus...

> *He opens his arms to embrace her. She grabs him by the tunic and tosses him toward the door.*

PENELOPE. Inside.

TELEMACHUS. But, Mother!

PENELOPE. Now. We need to talk.

> *Exit PENELOPE and TELEMACHUS. The SUITORS stand bewildered.*

NOEMON. Well, that was our chance.

EURYMACHUS. What do we do now?

> *Pause.*

ANTINOUS. More wine here!

> *Exit.*

ACT 2, SCENE 8

"Lying to Penelope"

Penelope's private sanctuary.

Enter PENELOPE and TELEMACHUS.

PENELOPE. What is wrong with you?

TELEMACHUS. Mother, listen—

PENELOPE. I told you I needed you here. And the next thing I know, you've disappeared, without so much as a word of warning or a reason why. Do you know I very nearly went insane? Nearly gave in to those brutes? That's what happens to a mother when she thinks her child is dead.

TELEMACHUS. I know. I'm sorry, Mother. But I couldn't wait around here anymore. I had to know what became of father.

PENELOPE. Well? What became of him? Is he dead?

TELEMACHUS. As good as dead.

PENELOPE. What does that mean?

TELEMACHUS. He's trapped on an island, held captive by the nymph Calypso.

PENELOPE. So he's with another woman.

TELEMACHUS. Against his will.

PENELOPE. How do you know that?

TELEMACHUS. I don't. But whether it's by force or by choice, the result is the same. He's not coming home. We have to face it, Mother. We have to move on.

PENELOPE. And how do you propose I do that?

TELEMACHUS. I have an idea...

> *Exit TELEMACHUS and PENELOPE.*

> *In another chamber, EURYCLEIA tends to ODYSSEUS.*

EURYCLEIA (*handing him a damp cloth*). Hold this on the cut above your eye. That's it.

ODYSSEUS. Thank you, Miss.

EURYCLEIA. Did they hit you anywhere else?

ODYSSEUS. My shin hurts. I think it may be bleeding.

EURYCLEIA. Let's see. I don't see any blood here, maybe it's—

She stops, suddenly, in shock.

ODYSSEUS. What?

EURYCLEIA. That scar… I know that scar.

ODYSSEUS. Do you?

EURYCLEIA. He was just a boy of twelve. His father had taken him hunting for the first time. He was so excited. But when they came home he was in his father's arms, crying. "Wild boar got him," his father said, and left him with my mother. I watched her clean and bandage it. A crooked, bleeding gash across his shin… (*realizing*) Master!

ODYSSEUS. Shhhh.

EURYCLEIA. Master, is it really you?

ODYSSEUS. Shhhh.

EURYCLEIA. But what have they done to you? You've aged so much!

ODYSSEUS. A disguise, given by the goddess. Eurycleia, listen to me. Do you wish to see me king again?

EURYCLEIA. Of course!

ODYSSEUS. Then you must help me. In a moment, the mistress will go out in the courtyard to announce a contest of all the suitors. I will be there, in this disguise. When I give a signal, I need you and your people to lock all the doors. Leave the courtyard, and lock us in. Understood?

EURYCLEIA. Yes, Master. But… does Mistress Penelope know you're here?

ODYSSEUS. No. And we are not to tell her until the work is done…

Exit.

ACT 2, SCENE 9

"The Purge"

The courtyard of Odysseus' house. PENELOPE stands at the front, addressing the SUITORS. ODYSSEUS, TELEMACHUS, and EUMAEUS are present.

PENELOPE. After speaking with my son, I have come to the conclusion that choosing one of you will be better than having to live with all of you.

The SUITORS cheer.

ANTINOUS. I knew she'd come around.

PENELOPE. Therefore, I propose a contest. As you know, my late husband was a skilled archer. This was the bow he used. It has not been strung since he left. The first man who can string it will win my hand.

All of the SUITORS plead with PENELOPE to go first.

PENELOPE. Eurymachus will go first.

SUITORS. Awww!

EURYMACHUS tries to string the bow, but can't.

NOEMON. Weakling! Here, let me have a try.

Music. Various SUITORS try to string the bow. Their turns get shorter as the frustration grows. It devolves into a tug-of-war over the bow. With a cry of rage, ANTINOUS pushes them all away and tries desperately to string the bow himself.

ANTINOUS. I don't understand. Why won't it work?

PENELOPE. It's as I thought. None of you has proven worthy.

EURYMACHUS. I can get it, Penelope. Just give me one more try.

NOEMON. My hands were sweaty before, but now they're dry!

PENELOPE. You failed. Clearly I must devise a new contest more suited to men of your caliber.

Exit PENELOPE.

ANTINOUS. I see now. It was a trick! She shortened the bowstring to make us look like fools.

MELANTHUS. Yeah! No man alive could string that thing.

ODYSSEUS. I bet I could.

ANTINOUS. You? Ha!

NOEMON. Now, now, Antinous. Let the geezer have his moment. We could all use a laugh.

> The SUITORS agree.

BIAS. Go on, old man. Give it a try.

> ODYSSEUS climbs up on the platform. As he picks up the bow, ATHENA appears next to him.

ODYSSEUS. Goddess!

ATHENA. Don't worry. Only you can see me.

ODYSSEUS. Is it time?

ATHENA. Not yet.

ELATUS. Who's he talking to?

LEOCRITUS. He's mad!

ATHENA. I've brought you one last gift.

ODYSSEUS. What is it?

ATHENA. First, string the bow.

ANTINOUS. What's taking so long, old timer?

THOAS. String the bloody bow!

ATHENA. String it.

> ODYSSEUS strings the bow. The SUITORS gasp.

MELANTHUS. What in the world?

ELATUS. How'd he do that?

NOEMON. He can't be that strong. There must be some trick to it.

ATHENA (*holding out her empty hands as if holding something long and thin*). Now take this.

ODYSSEUS. I don't understand. There's nothing there.

ATHENA. Just because you can't see it doesn't mean it isn't real.

> *ODYSSEUS takes the invisible arrow and nocks it.*

ODYSSEUS. Now, Eurycleia.

> *EURYCLEIA and the SERVANTS exit, locking the doors behind them.*

ANTINOUS. What is happening right now?

> *He takes aim at the crowd of the SUITORS. They laugh.*

EURYMACHUS. I think you need an arrow for that thing!

> *ODYSSEUS lets loose the bowstring. Sound of an arrow cutting through the air. The SUITORS laugh until THOAS falls to his knees. The SUITORS step away in horror.*

MELANTHUS. Thoas…

ELATUS. He's dead.

NOEMON. That doesn't even make sense!

ANTINOUS. Who are you?

> *ATHENA taps ODYSSEUS and he pulls off his cloak.*

ANTINOUS. No… It can't be… Odysseus?

EUMAEUS. Well don't just stand there. Bow to your king.

ANTINOUS. Kill him!

> *A SUITOR attacks ODYSSEUS, but TELEMACHUS and EUMAEUS stab him.*

ANTINOUS. Run!

> *The SUITORS go for the doors.*

POLYBUS. It's barred!

BIAS. This one's bolted!

ANTINOUS. What do you want? We'll give you gold, riches, anything you ask!

ODYSSEUS. But I asked for bread. And you denied me. Every. Last. One of you.

An epic battle ensues.

ODYSSEUS, TELEMACHUS, and EUMAEUS slaughter the SUITORS. A few SUITORS, including EURYMACHUS and ANTINOUS, get their hands on swords and try to fight back. One by one, they are slain. The last one alive is ANTINOUS. He and ODYSSEUS duel until ANTINOUS is brought to sword point.

ANTINOUS. Please, have mercy, Odysseus! Or, barring that, a proper burial.

ODYSSEUS. I'll grant you the second.

He runs him through.

ODYSSEUS. There. It's finished…

Lights fade.

ACT 2, SCENE 10
"Reunited"

The beach. PENELOPE stands looking out at the waves. Upstage, a tree stands on what used to be the ship's deck.

Enter ODYSSEUS and TELEMACHUS. ODYSSEUS walks up to PENELOPE.

PENELOPE turns and sees him. At first she makes to move toward him. He reciprocates. But then she steps back and draws a knife.

PENELOPE. No. Get away from me.

TELEMACHUS. Mother, is that any way to treat your husband? It's father.

PENELOPE. We don't know that yet.

TELEMACHUS. But we do! He killed the suitors. Come and see!

ODYSSEUS. Telemachus, leave us a moment. Your mother will know me soon enough.

Exit TELEMACHUS.

ODYSSEUS. Is it the clothes? I know they're a little shabby.

PENELOPE. He said the suitors were dead.

ODYSSEUS. They're dead.

PENELOPE. You can't have killed them by yourself.

ODYSSEUS. Not by myself. I had help from my son, from my servants, from a grey-eyed goddess... and from my wife, who has waited for me all this time.

PENELOPE. And how do you think I've managed that? Certainly not by throwing myself into the arms of every impostor that comes along.

ODYSSEUS. Impostor? Penelope, it's me, your Odysseus.

PENELOPE. My Odysseus is dead. His bones are at the bottom of the sea.

ODYSSEUS. Come here.

PENELOPE. Stay back.

Enter EURYCLEIA.

EURYCLEIA. Mistress, what are you doing?

ODYSSEUS. Eurycleia, I don't think my wife and I will be sharing a bed tonight. Have the servants find me somewhere else to sleep.

PENELOPE. No, Eurycleia. He's our guest. Move my bed into a different chamber and I'll sleep on the floor.

EURYCLEIA (*starting to leave*). Yes, Mistress.

ODYSSEUS. Wait. Oh, you are clever, Penelope. They say I'm the clever one, but it was you all along. You can't move the bed. It's impossible.

PENELOPE (*taking his hand*). Why?

ODYSSEUS (*leading her up to the tree*). Because our bed is built into the earth. And from its headboard grows an olive tree. I built that bed for us, with my own hands. And only you and I have ever seen it.

They sit down together on either side of the tree.

ODYSSEUS. Well?

PENELOPE (*through tears*). I always knew you'd come back.

Lights fade.

CURTAIN

Check out **lighthouseplays.com** to see our full library of plays,
from *A Christmas Carol* to *Frankenstein* and more!

Book and cover design by Laura Wimer: **iamlew.com**

Cover illustrations by Kate Zaremba: **katezarembacompany.com**

Published in partnership with Can't Not: **cantnotproductions.com**

Made in the USA
Middletown, DE
06 January 2020